A Manual

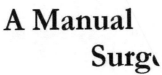

Surgery

*Or, Hints on the Emergencies of Field,
Camp and Hospital*

Samuel David Gross

APPLEWOOD BOOKS
Bedford, Massachusetts

A Manual of Military Surgery
was originally published in
1861

9781429015202

For a free copy of our current print catalog featuring our bestselling books, write to:

APPLEWOOD BOOKS
P.O. Box 365
Bedford, MA 01730

For more complete listings, visit us on the web at:
awb.com

Prepared for publishing by HP

A MANUAL

OF

MILITARY SURGERY;

OR,

HINTS ON THE EMERGENCIES OF

FIELD, CAMP, AND HOSPITAL PRACTICE.

ILLUSTRATED WITH WOOD-CUTS.

BY S. D. GROSS, M.D.,

PROF. OF SURGERY IN THE JEFFERSON MEDICAL COLLEGE OF PHILADELPHIA.

[SECOND EDITION.]

———

"L'occasion est urgente, le jugement difficile."
"For want of timely care, millions have died of medicable wounds."

———

PHILADELPHIA:
J. B. LIPPINCOTT & CO.
1862.

TO

SAMUEL WIESSELL GROSS, M.D.,

LECTURER ON ANATOMY AND SURGERY,

And one of the Editors of the North American Medico-Chirurgical Review,

THIS LITTLE VOLUME,

DESIGNED TO MITIGATE SOME OF THE HORRORS

OF THE CIVIL WAR

NOW IMPENDING OVER

OUR ONCE HAPPY AND GLORIOUS COUNTRY,

IS AFFECTIONATELY INSCRIBED

BY

THE AUTHOR

PREFACE.

THE sole object which prompts me to publish this little book is an ardent desire to be useful to the young physicians who have so hurriedly entered the volunteer service, perhaps not always with a full knowledge of the weighty responsibilities of their position. It treats, very succinctly, of various matters not generally discussed, except in large and ponderous volumes, inaccessible in the camp and on the battle-field. It is essentially a book for emergencies; portable, easy of reference, always at hand. The substance of it was originally intended as an article for the July number of the NORTH AMERICAN MEDICO-CHIRURGICAL REVIEW, and it was not until I had made considerable progress in its composition that the idea suggested itself to my mind that it might, if published separately, be of service to a part of my profession at this particular juncture in our public affairs.

I pray the young men into whose hands this Manual may happen to fall, to be careful of the health and lives of the poor soldiers committed to their professional keeping. I exhort them to perform their duty as skillful surgeons and physicians, as men of courage, and as Christians, in order that, when they return to their homes and their friends, after the tumult and perils of war shall be over—if war there should unfortunately be—they may be able to render a good account of their stewardship, and so entitle themselves to their country's benediction.

I would also exhort them, in a special manner, to take good care, not only of the lives of their countrymen, but also of their limbs, mutilated in battle. Conservative surgery has, at the present day, claims of paramount importance upon the attention of every military practitioner; for, in the language of good old George Herbert,

> Man is all symmetrie,
> Full of proportion, one limbe to another,
> And all to all the world besides;   .
> Each part calls the furthest brother;
> For head with foot hath private amitie;
> And both with moons and tides.

S. D. GROSS.

PHILADELPHIA, MAY, 1861.

CONTENTS.

(vii)

A MANUAL

OF

MILITARY SURGERY.

CHAPTER I.

Historical Sketch of Military Surgery.

THE duties and requirements of military are essentially similar to those of civil surgery. It is founded upon the same knowledge of anatomy, medicine, and the associate sciences; it demands the same qualifications, physical, moral, and intellectual. The difference consists in the application of our knowledge rather than in its range or depth. The civil surgeon remains at home; the military follows the army, examines recruits for the public service, and superintends the health of the troops. If the former is well educated, he will be quite as competent, at any time, as

2

the latter to perform these duties; for the emergencies of civil are often not less trying than those of military practice, although they may not be on so large a scale.

The best civil have often also been the best military surgeons.   In proof of this assertion it is necessary only to refer to the names of Paré, Wiseman, Schmucker, Kern, Larrey, Guthrie, Charles Bell, Alcock, Thomson, Ballingall, and Macleod, of Europe; or to those of Rush, Jones, Thacher, Mann, and Horner of our own country.

Military surgery occupies, at the present day, a deservedly high rank in the estimation both of the profession and of the public. The war in the Crimea, the mutiny in India, and the recent convulsions in Italy, all attended with so much waste of blood and life, have attracted to it the universal attention of the profession; and the revolutionary movements now in progress in our own country invest it with a new and a fearful interest to every American physician.   Its praises have been sung by Homer, and, in all ages of the world, governments have extended to it a fostering hand. As a distinct branch, however, of the healing art, it dates back no fur-

ther than the early part of the sixteenth century, when it was inaugurated by Ambrose
Paré, by the publication of his treatise on
"Gunshot Wounds," the fruits of his observations in the French army in Italy. This man,
who was surgeon to four successive kings, was
an eye-witness of the numerous French campaigns, from 1536 down to the battle of
Moncontour, in 1569, a period of thirty-
three years. His popularity, both as a civil
and military surgeon, was, up to that time,
without a parallel. The soldiers worshiped
him; and the success of more than one siege,
as well of one battle, was due almost exclu-
sively to the wonderful influence of his presence. His treatise on "Gunshot Wounds"
appeared toward the middle of the sixteenth
century, and, after having passed through
various editions, was ultimately incorporated
in his surgical writings, published nearly a
quarter of a century later.

In England, the earliest work on military
surgery was that of Thomas Gale, entitled a
"Treatise on Gunshot Wounds," designed
chiefly to confute the errors of some of his
contemporaries, respecting the supposed pois-
onous nature of these lesions. Gale was born

in 1507, and after having served in the army
of King Henry VIII., at Montrieul, and also
in that of King Philip, at St. Quintin, finally
settled at London, where he acquired great
distinction in his profession. In 1639 appeared the work of J. Woodall, "The Surgeon's
Mate ; or, Military and Domestic Surgery."
He was surgeon under Queen Elizabeth, by
whom he was sent to France, along with the
troops that were dispatched to the assistance
of Henry IV. and Lord Willoughby.   In
1676, Richard Wiseman, sergeant-surgeon to
King Charles II., published his famous "Chirurgical Treatises," one of which was expressly devoted to the consideration of gunshot wounds. Two years after this a treatise
on gunshot wounds was published at London,
by John Brown, also surgeon to Charles. He
was a man of eminence, and served with much
credit in the Dutch war of 1665. The next
English work on military surgery appeared
in 1744, from the pen of John Ranby, sergeant-surgeon to George II., under the title of
"The Method of Treating Gunshot Wounds."
After Ranby came the imperishable work of
John Hunter, familiar to every reader of English surgical literature. The part relating to

gunshot wounds was founded upon his observations made while serving as staff-surgeon at Belleisle and in Portugal, and is one of the most precious legacies of the last century, near the close of which it appeared.

The present century has supplied quite a number of works on military surgery, as is shown by the valuable publications of Larrey, Hennen, Hecker, Augustin, Guthrie, Thomson, Hutchinson, Ballingall, Baudens, and others, which have contributed so much to the elevation of this department of the healing art. Some of these works have been reissued in this country, and have acquired a wide celebrity.

We must not forget, in this rapid enumeration of works on military surgery, the "Manuel de Chirurgien d'Armée" of Baron Percy, published at the commencement of the revolutionary war in France. It is a model of what such a treatise ought to be.

The only work on this department of science yet furnished in this country, is that of the late Dr. James Mann, published at Dedham, Massachusetts, in 1816. It is entitled "Medical Sketches of the Campaigns of 1812, '13, and '14," and forms a closely-printed volume of upwards of three hundred octavo pages.

The latest treatise on this subject in the English language is that of Dr. George H. B. Macleod, now Professor of Surgery at Glasgow, entitled "Notes on the Surgery of the War in the Crimea; with Remarks on the Treatment of Gunshot Wounds." It is a work of intense interest, written with great ability by an accurate and diligent observer, and is worthy of a place in every medical library. To this work frequent reference will be made in the following pages.

To Dr. Lewis Stromeyer, Physician of the Royal Hanoverian Army, we are indebted for the most recent German work on military surgery. It was issued in 1858, under the title of "Maximen der Kriegsheilkunst," in two duodecimo volumes, to which a Supplement was added in the early part of the present year. A more valuable contribution to this department of surgery could hardly be imagined.

Besides the above more recent works, the reader should carefully study the "Principles of Military Surgery," by the late Dr. John Hennen, one of the most zealous and distin-

guished military surgeons that Great Britain
has yet produced; a man of vast experience,
and of the most enlightened views upon everything which he has touched with his pen.

Perhaps the most systematic work on the
subject in the English language is that of Sir
George Ballingall, entitled "Outlines of Military Surgery," the last edition of which,
the fourth, appeared only recently at Edin-
burgh, where the author held for many years
the chair of military surgery, for a long time,
we believe, the only one in Great Britain.
It is a production of much merit, and is des-
tined to maintain a very high rank in this
species of literature.

The works of the late Mr. George Guthrie
also deserve attentive study; they are written
with great clearness and ability, and embody
the results of an immense experience, acquired
during many years of arduous and faithful
labor and observation in the British army. I
have always regarded the works of this great
man as among the most valuable contributions,
not only to military surgery, but to surgery
in general, in the English language.

With these works before him, the student
of military surgery cannot fail to make him-

self in a short time perfectly familiar with
everything pertaining to the subjects of which
they treat. He should also provide himself
with a copy of the excellent little volume entitled "Hints on the Medical Examination of
Recruits for the Army," by the late Dr.
Thomas Henderson, formerly Professor of
Medicine in Columbia College, Washington
City. A new edition of it was published a
few years ago by Dr. Richard H. Coolidge,
of the United States army.

Although we have long had one of the most
respectable and thoroughly organized army
and naval medical staffs in the world, our country has, nevertheless, not produced one great
military surgeon; simply, it may be presumed,
because no opportunity has occurred since the
establishment of our government, in which the
men in the public service could distinguish
themselves. Their aid has been required in
the duello and in skirmishes rather than in
great battles, such as have so often characterized the movements of the armies of the
Old World. We make no exception in this
remark in favor even of the battles that were
fought during the Revolution, and during our
Late War, as it has usually been designated,

with Great Britain. Those engagements were, for the most part, comparatively bloodless. Happily living under a flag which, until recently, commanded alike the respect and the admiration of all nations, belonging to a government which was at peace with all foreign powers, the medical and surgical staffs of the public service had little else to do than to prescribe for such diseases as are incident to civil practice. America has never witnessed, and we trust in God she never may witness, such carnage as that which attended the footsteps of Napoleon at the Bridge of Lodi, at Leipzig, at Dresden, and at Waterloo; or which, more recently, characterized the exploits of the English, French, and Russian forces in the Crimea; or of the French, Italian, and Austrian armies in Italy; or of the English soldiers during the late rebellion in India. Nor has she ever been engaged in one great naval battle similar to that of La Hogue, Toulon, Trafalgar, or Aboukir. A number of highly respectable physicians accompanied our army to Mexico, but they returned without any special laurels, and without any substantial contributions to military medicine and surgery.

CHAPTER II.

Importance of Military Surgery.

IT is impossible for any civilized nation to place too high an estimate upon this branch of the public service. Without the aid of a properly organized medical staff, no army, however well disciplined, could successfully carry on any war, even when it is one, as that which is now impending over us, of a civil character. No men of any sober reflection would enlist in the service of their country, if they were not positively certain that competent physicians and surgeons would accompany them in their marches and on the field of battle, ready to attend to their diseases and accidents. Hence military surgery, or, more correctly speaking, military medicine and surgery, has always occupied a deservedly high rank in public estimation.

Dionis, a surgeon far in advance of his age, in referring to the value of medical services to soldiers, exclaims, with a burst of eloquence: "We must then allow the neces-

sity of chirurgery, which daily raises many
persons from the brink of the grave. How
many men has it cured in the army! How
many great commanders would have died of
their ghastly wounds without its assistance!
Chirurgery triumphs in armies and in sieges.
'Tis true that its empire is owned: 'tis there
that its effects, and not words, express its
eulogium.''

The confidence reposed by soldiers in the
skill and humanity of their surgeon has often
been of signal service in supporting them,
when exhausted by hunger and fatigue, in
their struggles to repel the advancing foe, or
in successfully maintaining a siege when the
prospect of speedy surrender was at hand.
Who that is versed in the history of our art
does not remember with what enthusiasm and
resolve Ambrose Paré, the father of French
surgery, inspired the souls of the half-starved
and desponding garrison at Metz, in 1552,
when besieged by 100,000 men under the
personal command of Charles V.? Sent
thither by his sovereign, he was introduced
into the city during the night by an Italian
captain; and the next morning, when he

showed himself upon the breach, he was received with shouts of welcome. "We shall not die," the soldiers exclaimed, "even though wounded; Paré is among us." The defense from this time was conducted with renewed vigor, and the French army ultimately completely triumphed, through the sole influence of this illustrious surgeon.

No man in the French army under Napoleon rendered so many and such important services to the French nation as Larrey, the illustrious surgeon who accompanied that mighty warrior in his various campaigns, everywhere animating the troops and doing all in his power to save them from the destructive effects of disease and injury. His humanity and tenderness were sublime; and so highly was his conduct, as an honest, brave, and skillful surgeon, appreciated by Napoleon, that he bequeathed him a large sum, with the remark that "Larrey was the most virtuous man he had ever known."

CHAPTER III.

Qualifications and Duties of Military Surgeons.

IT is of paramount importance that none but men of the best talent and of the highest education should be received into the public service. Rigid as the examinations of the army and naval medical boards already are, there is need of increased rigor, in order that none may be admitted who are not thoroughly prepared for the discharge of their responsible duties. Equal vigilance should be exercised in regard to the introduction of physicians and surgeons into the volunteer service. Every regiment should be provided with an able medical head, a man ready for every emergency, however trying or unexpected; a man skilled in the diagnosis and treatment of diseases, and competent to perform any operation, whether small or large, on the spur of the moment. To do this, he must be more than a mere physician; he must be both physician and surgeon, in the true sense of the terms, otherwise he will be unfit, totally un-

3

fit, for his position: He must have been
educated in the modern schools; be of un-
doubted courage, prompt to act, willing to
assume responsibility, humane and sympa-
thizing, urbane and courteous in his manners;
in short, a medical gentleman, as well as a
medical philosopher,—not hesitating, if need
be, to perform the most menial services, and
to do all he can to preserve the health and
the lives of the soldiers committed to his care.
The white-gloved gentry, such as figured in
some of the regiments that went to Mexico,
have no business in the service; their time
can be much better spent in the discharge of
their domestic duties, in the practice of their
neighborhood, and in the contemplation, at a
distance, of the miseries of war.

It is much to be feared that, from the rapid
manner in which our volunteers have been hur-
ried together, many medical men, old as well
as young, have already been admitted into the
service utterly unfit for the office. If this be
the case, let our authorities, warned by the
past, be more circumspect in regard to the
future. Above all, let them see that the
medical staffs of the brave volunteers of the
country be not defiled by charlatans and un-

worthy men, between whom and the regular practitioners there cannot possibly be any professional, much less social intercourse, either in civil or military practice. The medical men should be on the best possible terms with each other; all causes of discord and bickering among themselves should be studiously obviated, and speedily suppressed, if, unfortunately, they should arise. Concert of action on the part of the medical corps is indispensable to the success of the medical operations of an army.

Every regimental surgeon should have at least two assistants in time of peace, or during the inactivity of the troops under his charge; when on active duty, on the contrary, the number should at least be double, especially in the face of an anticipated bloody engagement. These assistants should be selected solely with reference to their competency; they should, like the principal, be eminently intelligent, and ready, in case of emergency, to perform any operation that occasion may demand. Every brigade should have its brigade surgeon, who should exercise a supervisory control over the regimental surgeons, principals as well as assistants, as every State should have its surgeon-general, or medical-director, whose duty it should be to superintend the whole medical arrangements, seeing that the candidates for the medical department of the service be subjected to a rigid examination, attending to the purchase of medicines and instruments, providing suitable nurses, inspecting the quarters, stores, and provisions; that nothing of an unwholesome character may find its way into the ranks, pointing out the proper location of camps, and the construction of hospitals, and giving general instructions in regard to military hygiene, or the best means of avoiding disease and accident.

Prior to every engagement at all likely to be severe or serious, a proper number of men should be detailed for the purpose of rendering prompt assistance to the wounded, and carrying them off the field of battle to the hospitals or tents erected for their accommodation and treatment. Unless this be done as a preliminary step, much suffering will inevitably be the consequence, if not great confusion, highly prejudicial to the issue of the combat. So fully aware are the leaders and sub-commanders of our armies of this fact that they never permit any man to fall out

of the ranks, during an engagement, to perform this service.

While the battle is progressing it is the duty
of the surgeon and of his assistants to remain
in the rear of the combatants, as much as possible out of harm's way, but at the same time
ready and on the watch to render the promptest
possible aid. They must be Argus-eyed, and
in the full possession of their wits. One of
the leading differences between military and
civil practice is the instantaneous action so
often demanded by the one, and the delay so
frequently admitted by the other.

The first duty of every surgeon is to the
officers and men of his own corps; but on
the field of battle, or soon after the battle is
over, he is often brought in contact with the
members of other regiments, or even with the
wounded of the enemy; and under such circumstances the dictates of humanity, not less
than the usages of war, demand that he should
render his services wherever they may be
likely to be useful. The medical officers, of
the contending parties sometimes meet upon
such occasions, and, when this is the case,
their conduct should invariably be character-

ized by the courtesy of the gentleman, not the
asperity of the enemy. They should not forget that they are brethren of the same noble
profession, acting in the capacity of minister-
ing angels to the sick and the dying. Country and cause alike should be forgotten in gene-
rous deeds.

By the usages of war in all civilized countries, the surgeons are always respected by
the enemy if, during an engagement, they
happen to fall accidentally into their hands.
Their lives are regarded as sacred, the more
so, as they are comparatively defenseless.
They are not, however, during the rage and
smoke of the battle-field, always easily distin-
guishable from the other officers, or even the
common soldiers. The green sash, their dis-
tinctive badge of office, does not always afford
them immunity, because it is not always recognized; and it is worthy of consideration
whether, as an additional safeguard, the word
"surgeon" should not be embroidered in legi-
ble characters upon a piece of cloth, to be
thrown across the chest in time of battle.
The significance of such a badge could not be
mistaken by friend or foe, and would be the
means of saving many valuable lives.

CHAPTER IV.

Medical Equipments, Stores, and Hospitals.

EVERY regiment, or body of military men, should be amply provided, in time of war, with the means of conveying the wounded and disabled from the field of battle. For this purpose suitable carriages and litters should constantly be in readiness. The carriages should be built in the form of light wagons, drawn each by two horses; with low wheels, easy springs, and a large, wide body, furnished with a soft mattress and pillows, and capable of accommodating not less than eight or ten persons, while arrangements might be made at the side for seating a number more, as in the French *voiture*. As a means of protection against the sun and the rain, it should have a light cover of oil-cloth or canvas.

A great number of *litters*, or bearers, will be found described in treatises on military surgery; but I am not acquainted with any

which combine so much simplicity and cheap-
ness, with lightness and convenience, as one
which, after a good deal of reflection, I have
just devised, and of which the accompanying
sketch affords a good illustration. It consists

 of two equal parts, connected
at the ends by stout hinges,
the arrangement being such as
to permit of their being folded
for more easy transportation
on the field of battle. Each
part has a side piece of wood,
three feet four inches long, by
two inches in depth, and an
inch and a half in thickness,
the free extremity terminating
in a slightly curved handle.
The side pieces are united by
four traverses, and the entire
frame is covered with ducking,
twenty-four inches in width. Thus constructed,
the apparatus is not only very light, so that
any one may easily carry it, or, indeed, even
three or four at a time, but remarkably convenient both for the transportation of patients, and for lifting them in and out of the

wagons, which should always be at hand
during an engagement. Moreover, by means
of side straps, provided with buckles, it will
answer extremely well for a bed-chair, so necessary in sickness and during convalescence,
the angle of flexion of the two pieces thus
admitting of ready regulation. In carrying
the wounded off the field, the labor may
easily be performed by two men, especially
if they use shoulder-straps to diffuse the
weight of the burden. The body, in hot
weather, might be protected with an oil-
cloth, while the face might be shielded from
the sun with a veil or handkerchief. A pillow for the head can be made with the coat
of one of the carriers.

Besides these means, every regiment should
be furnished with an *ambulance*, or, as the
term literally implies, a movable hospital, that
is, a place for the temporary accommodation
and treatment of the wounded on the field of
battle. It should be arranged in the form of
a tent, and be provided with all the means
and appliances necessary for the prompt succor of the sufferers. The materials of which it
consists should be as light as possible, possess

every facility for rapid packing and erection, and be conveyed from point to point by a wagon set apart for this object. The ambulance, for the invention and improvement of which we are indebted to two eminent French military surgeons, Percy and Larrey, is indispensable in every well-regulated army.

This temporary hospital should be placed in an open space, convenient to water, and upon dry ground, with arrangements for the free admission of air and light, which, next to pure air, is one of the most powerful stimulants in all cases of accident attended with excessive prostration. The direct rays of the sun, in hot weather, must of course be excluded, and it may even be necessary, as in injuries of the head and eye, to wrap the patient in complete darkness. A properly-regulated temperature is also to be maintained, a good average being about 68° of Fahrenheit's thermometer.

As engagements are sometimes begun after dark, or are continued into the night, an adequate supply of wax candles should be provided, as they will be found indispensable both in field and hospital practice in performing operations and dressing wounds and fractures. Torches, too, will frequently be needed, especially in collecting and transporting the wounded. Bed-pans, feeding-cups, spoons, syringes, and other appliances usually found in the sick chamber, will form a necessary part of the furniture of such an establishment.

The object of the ambulance is, as already stated, to afford prompt succor to the wounded. Here their lighter injuries are speedily dressed, and the more grave subjected to the operations necessary for their cure. In due time, the former are sent back to the ranks, while the rest are conveyed to suitable lodgings or to permanent hospitals.

As soon as practicable, after the hurry and confusion attendant upon a combat are over, the surgeon should classify the wounded and disabled, taking care that those laboring under similar lesions are not brought in close contact; lest, witnessing each other's sufferings, they should be seized with fatal despondency.

Larrey, in order to meet the exigencies of the grand army in Italy, constructed a *flying*

ambulance; an immense, and, at first sight, a
very cumbersome establishment. It consisted
of twelve light wagons, on easy springs, for
the transportation of the wounded; some with
two, others with four wheels. The frame of
the former, which were designed for flat, level
countries, resembled an elongated cube, curved
on the top; it had two small windows on each
side, with a folding-door in front and behind.
The floor of the body, separable and movable
on rollers, was covered with a mattress and
bolster. Handles were secured to it laterally,
through which the sashes of the soldiers were
passed in lifting the sick in and out of the
carriage, when, on account of the weather,
their wants could not be relieved on the
ground. Each vehicle was thirty-two inches
wide, and was drawn by two horses; it could
conveniently accommodate two patients at full
length, and was furnished with several side-
pockets for such articles as might be needed
for the sufferers.

The large carriage, drawn by four horses,
and designed for rough and hilly roads, was
constructed upon the same principle as the
small; it had four wheels, and could accom-

modate four persons. The left side of the
body had two long sliding-doors, extending
almost its whole length, so as to permit the
wounded to be laid in a horizontal position.

These carriages were used for conveying the
wounded from the field of battle to the hospitals of the lines, and combined, it is said,
solidity with lightness and elegance.

The number of men attached to the flying
ambulance was 113, embracing a soldier's
guard with twelve men on horseback, a
quartermaster-general, a surgeon-major, with
his two assistants and twelve mates, a police
officer, and a number of servants. The flying
ambulance was, in fact, a costly and imposing
establishment, devised by the humanity and
ingenuity of the great and good Larrey, who
could never do too much for the wounded soldier, and whose presence, like that of his illustrious countryman, Paré, always served to
animate the French troops. At one time
three divisions of the flying ambulance,
equipped upon this grand scale, were upon
the field in different parts of Italy.

It is not deemed necessary, in a work like
this, to give an account of the construction of

4

hospitals, properly so termed; for, with the railroad and steamboat facilities which we now possess, there can be little difficulty in obtaining comfortable accommodations for the sick and wounded soldiers. Lodgings can almost always be procured, in nearly every portion of the country where a battle is likely to be fought, in houses, churches, and barns. Temporary sheds might easily be erected in a few hours, with such arrangements as would serve for the more pressing wants of the wounded. The chief points to be attended to, in their construction, are sufficient elevation of the ground floor for the free circulation of air, windows for light and ventilation, and such a position of the fire-place as not to annoy the inmates.

The *medical stores* of the military hospital, whether temporary or permanent, include medicines, instruments, and various kinds of apparatus, as bandages, oiled silk, and splints.

It would far transcend my limits were I to enter fully into all the details connected with these different topics. A few brief remarks under each head must suffice for my purpose.

1st. In regard to *medicines*, a few articles

only, well selected and arranged for ready
use, will be necessary. It is bad enough, in
all conscience, for a man to be severely shot
or stabbed, without physicking him to death.
Let him by all means have a chance for his
life, especially when he has already been
prostrated by shock and hemorrhage. Food
and drink, with opium and fresh air, will
then do him more good than anything else.
I shall enumerate the medicines upon which,
in my judgment, most reliance is to be placed
in this kind of practice, according to their
known effects upon the system.

1. Anodynes:—opium, morphia, and black
drop, or acetated tincture of opium.

2. Purgatives:—blue mass, colomel, rhu-
barb, jalap, compound extract of colocynth,
and sulphate of magnesia. Some of these
articles should be variously combined, and
put up in pill form for ready use.

3. Depressants:—tartrate of antimony and
potassa, ipecacuanha, and tincture of veratrum viride.

4. Diaphoretics:—antimony, ipecacuanha,
nitrate of potassa, morphia, and Dover's
powder.

5. Diuretics :—nitrate and carbonate of potassa, and colchicum.

6. Antiperiodics :—quinine and arsenic.

7. Anæsthetics :—chloroform and ether.

8. Stimulants :—brandy, gin, wine, and aromatic spirits of ammonia.

9. Astringents :—acetate of lead, perchloride of iron and alum, tannin, gallic acid, and nitrate of silver.

10. Escharotics :—nitric acid, acid nitrate of mercury, (Bennett's formula,) and Vienna paste.

2d. The surgical *armamentarium* should also be as simple as possible. It should embrace a small pocket case, with a screw catheter ; a full amputating case, with at least three tourniquets, two saws of different sizes, and several large bone-nippers ; and, lastly, a trephining case. Several silver catheters of different sizes, a stomach pump, small and large syringes, feeding-cups and bed-pans should also be put up.

3d. Under the head of *apparatus* may be included bandages, lint, linen, adhesive plaster, splints, cushions, wadding, and oiled silk.

The *bandages*, composed of tolerably stout

muslin, should be free from starch and selvage, well rolled, and, on an average, from two inches and a quarter to two inches and a half in width by eight yards in length. The bandage of Scultetus, very serviceable in compound fractures, can easily be made, as occasion may require, out of pieces of the common roller.

Of *lint*, the patent, or apothecary's, as it is termed, is the best, as it is soft and easily adapted to the parts to which it is intended to be applied. Old linen or muslin also answers sufficiently well. Charpie is now seldom used.

An abundance of *adhesive plaster*, put up in small cases, should be provided. Collodion will not be necessary.

Splints, of binders or trunk-makers' board, and of light wood, should find a place in every medical store, as frequent occasions occur for their use. In fractures of the lower extremity special apparatus may be required, which, however, as it is cumbrous and inconvenient to carry, may generally be prepared as it is needed.

Cushions are made of muslin, sewed in the

4*

form of bags, of variable size and shape, and filled with cotton, tow, saw-dust or sand. They are designed to equalize and ward off pressure in the treatment of fractures of the lower extremities.

Wadding is a most valuable article in surgical practice, both for lining splints and making pads, as well as in the treatment of burns and scalds, and cannot be dispensed with.

Oiled silk is a prominent article in the dressings of the present day; it preserves the heat and moisture of poultices and of warm water-dressings, at the same time that it protects the bed and body-clothes of the patient.

Oil-cloth, soft and smooth, is required in all cases of severe wounds and fractures, attended with much discharge.

Air-cushions should be put up in considerable numbers, as their use will be indispensable in all cases of disease and injury involving protracted confinement.

Bran and saw-dust will be found of great value in the treatment of compound fractures, ulcers, gangrene, and suppurating wounds, as an easy support for the injured limb and a means of excluding flies.

Medical *case-books* should be put up along with the other articles, for the accurate registration of the names of the sick and wounded, the nature of their lesions, and the results of treatment. The medical officers should also keep a faithful record of the state of the weather, the temperature of the air, the nature of the climate, the products of the soil, and the botany of the country through which they pass or in which they sojourn, together with such other matters as may be of professional or scientific interest. The knowledge thus acquired should be disseminated after their return for the benefit of their professional brethren.

Finally, in order to complete hospital equipments, well-trained *nurses* should be provided; for good nursing is indispensable in every case of serious disease, whatever may be its character. The importance of this subject, however, is now so well appreciated as not to require any special comments here.

The question as to whether this duty should be performed by men or women is of no ma-

terial consequence, provided it be well
done.   The eligibility of women for this
task was thoroughly tested in the Crimea,
through the agency of that noble-hearted
female, Florence Nightingale; and hundreds
of the daughters of our land have already
tendered their services to the government for
this object.   No large and well-regulated
hospital can get on without some male nurses,
and they are indispensable in camp and field
practice.

It is not my purpose here to point out the
qualities which constitute a good female nurse.
It will suffice to say that she should be keenly
alive to her duties, and perform them, however menial or distasteful, with promptness
and alacrity.   She must be tidy in her appearance, with a cheerful countenance, light
in her step, noiseless, tender and thoughtful
in her manners, perfect mistress of her feel-
ings, healthy, able to bear fatigue, and at
least twenty-two years of age.   Neither the
crinoline nor the silk dress must enter into
her wardrobe; the former is too cumbrous,
while the latter by its rustling is sure to fret
the patient and disturb his sleep.   Whisper-

ing and walking on tiptoe, as has been truly observed by Florence Nightingale, are an abomination in the sick chamber. Finally, a good nurse never fails to anticipate all, or nearly all, the more important wants of the sufferer.

Among the things to be specially attended to in nursing is *ventilation*. Persons visiting the sick must at once be struck with the difference of pure air in those chambers where a proper ventilation exists and those where the reverse is the case. To insure this the fresh air should always be admitted from a window not open directly on the bed, or causing the patient to be in a draught. Even in winter it is highly proper that fresh air should be admitted some time during the day when there is a good fire and the patient well protected by covering.

The pillows, bedding, and bedclothes should be well aired and often changed, as also the flannel, under-garments, and night-dress. To facilitate this, it is well, when the patient is very ill and unable to help himself, to have the shirt open all the way down in front, and buttoned up. The patient often escapes great

suffering and annoyance by this simple method.
Where there is a discharge from sores or when
water-dressings are applied to a limb, it is advisable to place the latter upon a folded sheet
with a thin, soft oil-cloth underneath. Great
tenderness and cleanliness should be used in
dressing wounds or sores. Old linen, muslin,
and lint should always be had in readiness for
this purpose. A great prejudice exists against
the use of muslin, the preference being generally given to linen, but the former is really
quite as good as the other, if it is soft and old.

In regard to the *cleanliness* of a sick-room,
it is advisable to use a mop occasionally for
the removal of flue from under the bed; when,
however, the patient is in too critical a situation for dampness, a few tea-leaves scattered
over the apartment will absorb the dust, and
can be quietly taken up with a hand-brush.
A frequent change of bed linen is very beneficial when practicable, and the clothes must
always be folded smoothly under the patient.
Great cleanliness should be observed in all
the surroundings of the sick-room, and particular attention must be paid to the glasses
in which medicine is given, in order to render

the doses as palatable as possible. The patient
should be washed whenever able, and his
teeth and hair well attended to. The body
seems infused with new vigor after such ablutions.

A frequent change of *posture* is immensely
conducive to the comfort and well-being of a
sick person, if performed with a careful eye
to his particular condition. Severe pain, loss
of sleep, excessive constitutional irritation,
and dreadful bed-sores are sure to follow, in
all low states of the system, if this precaution
be not duly heeded. No patient must have
his head suddenly raised, or be permitted to
lie high, when he is exhausted from shock,
hemorrhage, or sickness. Many lives have
been lost by this indiscretion.

The apartment must be free from noise,
the light should neither be too freely admitted
nor too much excluded, except in head and
eye affections, and the temperature must be
regulated by the thermometer, from 65° to
68° of Fahrenheit being a proper average.

As the patient acquires strength, he may
gradually sit up in bed, propped up at first
by pillows, and afterward by a bed-chair.

His food and drink, and also, at times, his
medicine, must be given from a feeding-cup
during the height of his disease, and a good
general rule is to administer them with great
regularity, provided this does not interfere
too much with his repose. If he is very weak,
and sleeps very long, it will be necessary to
wake him in order to give him nourishment;
but, in general, sleep is more refreshing than
food, and more beneficial than medicine. The
bed-pan and urinal of course find their appropriate sphere under such circumstances.

As the appetite and strength increase, the
patient is permitted to resume, though very
gradually, his accustomed diet, and to exercise
about the room, if not in the open air. After
severe accidents and protracted sickness, a
wise man will not bestir himself too soon or
too much, but court the fickle goddess of
health with becoming caution.

Dying patients should be carefully screened
from their neighbors, placed in the easiest
posture, have free access of air, and be not
disturbed by noise, loud talking, or the presence of persons not needed for their comfort.
As soon as the mortal struggle is over, the
body must be removed.

The *excretions* should be removed as speedily as possible from the apartment, and the vessels in which they are received immediately well scalded, the air being at the same time perfectly purified by ventilation, or ventilation and disinfectants.

Finally, the nurse must take care of herself. She must have rest, or she will soon break down. If she is obliged to be up all night, she should be spared in the day.

CHAPTER V.

Wounds and Other Injuries.

THE injuries inflicted in war are, in every respect, similar to those received in civil life. The most common and important are fractures, dislocations, bruises, sprains, burns, and the different kinds of wounds, as the incised, punctured, lacerated, and gunshot. With the nature, diagnosis, and mode of treatment of these lesions every army surgeon must, of course, be supposed to be familiar; and I shall therefore limit myself,

5

in the remarks which I am about to offer upon these subjects, to a few practical hints respecting their management on the field of battle and in the ambulance.

Most of the cases of *fractures* occurring on the field of battle are the result of gunshot injury, and are frequently, if not generally, attended by such an amount of injury to the soft parts and also to the bone as to demand amputation. The bone is often dreadfully comminuted, and consequently utterly unfit for preservation. The more simple fractures, on the contrary, readily admit of the retention of the limb, without risk to life.

In transporting persons affected with fractures, whether simple or complicated, the utmost care should be used to render them as comfortable as possible, by placing the injured limb in an easy position, and applying, if need be, on account of the distance to which they have to be carried, or the mode of conveyance, short side splints of binders' board, thin wood, as a shingle, or junks of straw, gently confined by a roller. For want of due precaution the danger to limb and life may be materially augmented. Permanent dressings should be applied at the earliest moment after the patient reaches the hospital. If the fracture be attended with splintering of the bone, all loose or detached pieces should at once be extracted; a proceeding which always wonderfully simplifies the case, inasmuch as it prevents, in great measure, the frightful irritation and suppuration which are sure to follow their retention. When this point has been properly attended to, the parts should be neatly brought together by suture, and covered with a compress wet with blood. As soon as inflammation arises—not before—water-dressings are employed. A suitable opening, or bracket, should be made in the apparatus to facilitate drainage and dressing.

Dislocations, accidents by no means common in military operations, are treated according to the general rules of practice; they should be speedily reduced, without the aid of chloroform, if the patient is faint or exhausted; with chloroform, if he is strong or reaction has been fully established. The operation may generally be successfully performed by simple manipulation; if, however,

the case is obstinate, pulleys may be necessary, or extension and counter-extension
made by judicious assistants.

Bruises, or contusions, unless attended with
pulpification, disorganization, or destruction
of the tissues, are best treated, at first, until
the pain subsides, with tepid water impregnated with laudanum and sugar of lead, or
some tepid spirituous lotion, and afterward,
especially if the patient be strong and robust,
with cold water, or cold astringent fluids.
If the injury be deep seated, extensive, and
attended with lesion of very important structures, the case will be a serious one, liable to
be followed by the worst consequences, requiring, perhaps, amputation.

Sprains are often accompanied with excessive pain and even severe constitutional symptoms. They should be treated with the free
use of anodynes and with warm water-dressings medicated with laudanum, or laudanum
and lead. The joint must be elevated and
kept at rest in an easy position. Leeches
may be applied, if they can be obtained;
otherwise, if plethora exist, blood may be
taken from the arm. By-and-by sorbefacient

liniments and friction come in play. Passive
motion should not be instituted too soon.

Among the accidents of war are *burns*, and,
occasionally, also scalds. The former may be
produced by ordinary fire or by the explosion
of gunpowder, either casual or from the blowing up of redoubts, bridges, houses or arsenals,
and vary from the most trivial to the most
serious lesions, involving a great extent of
surface or of tissue, and liable to be followed
by the worst consequences. Such injuries
always require prompt attention; for, apart
from the excessive pain and collapse which so
often accompany them, the longer they remain uncared for the more likely will they
be to end badly.

Various remedies have been proposed for
these injuries. I have myself always found
white-lead paint, such as that employed in
the arts, mixed with linseed oil to the consistence of very thick cream, and applied so as
to form a complete coating, the most soothing
and efficient means. The dressing is finished
by enveloping the parts in wadding, confined
by a moderately tight roller. It should not
be removed, unless there is much discharge or

swelling, for several days.   If vesicles exist,
they should previously be opened with a
needle or the point of a bistoury.   A lini-
ment or ointment of glycerin, lard or simple
cerate, and subnitrate of bismuth, as suggested by my friend, Professor T. G. Rich-
ardson, of New Orleans, is also an excellent
remedy, and may be used in the same manner
as the white-lead paint.   In the milder cases,
carded cotton, cold water, water and alcohol,
water and laudanum, or solutions of lead and
laudanum, generally afford prompt relief.
Amputation will be necessary when there is
extensive destruction of the muscles, bones,
or joints.   Reaction must be promoted by
the cautious use of stimulants; while pain is
allayed by morphia or laudanum given with
more than ordinary circumspection, lest it
induce fatal oppression of the brain.

  In burns from the explosion of *gunpowder*,
particles of this substance are often buried in
the skin, where, if it be not removed, they
leave disfiguring marks.   The best way to get
rid of them is to pick out grain after grain
with the point of a narrow-bladed bistoury or
cataract needle.

The subject of *wounds* is a most important one in regard to field practice, as these lesions are not only of frequent occurrence, but present themselves in every variety of form and extent. Their gravity is influenced by numerous circumstances which our space does not permit us to specify, but which the intelligent reader can readily appreciate. In many cases death is instantaneous, owing to shock, or shock and hemorrhage; in others it occurs gradually, with or without reaction, at a period of several hours, or, it may be, not under several days. Sometimes men are destroyed by shock, by, apparently, the most insignificant wound or injury, owing, not to want of courage, but to some idiosyncrasy.

The indications presented in all wounds, of whatever nature, are—1st, to relieve shock; 2dly, to arrest hemorrhage; 3dly, to remove foreign matter; 4thly, to approximate and retain the parts; and, 5thly, to limit the resulting inflammation.

1. It is not necessary to describe minutely the symptoms of *shock*, as the nature of the case is sufficiently obvious at first sight, from the excessive pallor of the countenance, the

weakened or absent pulse, the confused state
of the mind, the nausea, or nausea and vomiting, and the excessive bodily prostration. The
case must be treated promptly: by free access of fresh air and the use of the fan, by
loosening the dress or the removal of all sources
of constriction, by dashing cold water into
the face and upon the chest, by recumbency
of the head, and by a draught of cold water,
or water and spirits, wine or hartshorn, if the
patient can swallow; aided, if the case be urgent, by sinapisms to the region of the heart,
the inside of the thighs and the spine, and
stimulating injections, as brandy, turpentine,
mustard, or ammonia, in a few ounces of
water. No fluid must be put into the mouth
so long as the power of deglutition is gone,
lest some of it should enter the windpipe, and
so occasion suffocation. Whatever the cause of
the shock may have been, let the medical
attendant not fail to encourage the sufferer by
a kind and soothing expression, which is often
of more value in recalling animation than the
best cordials.

During an actual engagement, the medical
officers, as well as their servants, should carry

in their pockets such articles as the wounded
will be most likely to need on the field of battle, as brandy, aromatic spirits of hartshorn,
and morphia, put up in suitable doses.

2. The *hemorrhage* may be arterial or venous, or both arterial and venous, slight or
profuse, primary or secondary, external or
internal. The scarlet color and saltatory jet
will inform us when it is arterial; the purple
hue and steady flow, when it is venous.
When the wound is severe, or involving a
large artery or vein, or even middle-sized
vessels, the bleeding may prove fatal in a few
minutes, unless immediate assistance is rendered. Hundreds of persons die on the field
of battle from this cause. They allow their
life-current to run out, as water pours from
a hydrant, without an attempt to stop it by
thrusting the finger in the wound, or com-
pressing the main artery of the injured limb.
They perish simply from their ignorance,
because the regimental surgeon has failed to
give the proper instruction. It is not necessary that the common soldier should carry a
Petit's tourniquet, but every one may put
into his pocket a stick of wood, six inches

long, and a handkerchief or piece of roller, with a thick compress, and be advised how, where, and when they are to be used. By casting the handkerchief round the limb, and placing the compress over its main artery, he can, by means of the stick, produce such an amount of compression as to put at once an effectual stop to the hemorrhage. This simple contrivance, which has been instrumental in saving thousands of lives, constitutes what is called the *field tourniquet*. A fife, drum-stick, knife, or ramrod may be used, if no special piece of wood is at hand.

The most reliable means for arresting hemorrhage permanently is the *ligature*, of strong, delicate, well-waxed silk, well applied, with one end cut off close to the knot. Acupressure is hardly a proper expedient upon the battle-field, or in the ambulance, especially when the number of wounded is considerable. The rule invariably is to tie a wounded artery both above and below the seat of injury, lest recurrent bleeding should arise. Another equally obligatory precept is to ligature the vessel, if practicable, at the place whence the blood issues, by enlarging, if need be, the original wound. The main trunk of the artery should be secured only when it cannot be taken up at the point just mentioned. Lastly, it is hardly requisite to add that the operation should be performed, with the aid of the tourniquet, as early as possible, before the supervention of inflammation and swelling, which must necessarily obscure the parts and increase the surgeon's embarrassment, as well as the patient's pain and risk.

Venous hemorrhage usually stops spontaneously, or readily yields to compression, even when a large vein is implicated. The ligature should be employed only in the event of absolute necessity, for fear of inducing undue inflammation.

Torsion is unworthy of confidence in field practice, and the same is true of *styptics*, except when the hemorrhage is capillary, or the blood oozes from numerous points. The most approved articles of this kind are Monsel's salt, or the persulphate of iron and the perchloride of iron; the latter deserving the preference, on account of the superiority of its hemostatic properties. Alum and lead are inferior styptics.

Temporary *compression* may be made with the tourniquet, or a compress and a roller. It may be direct, as when the compress is applied to the orifice of the bleeding vessel, or indirect, as when it is applied to the trunk of the vessel, at some distance from the wound.

Constitutional treatment in hemorrhage is of paramount importance. It comprises perfect tranquillity of mind and body, cooling drinks, a mild, concentrated, nourishing diet, especially when there has been excessive loss of blood, anodynes to allay pain, induce sleep, and allay the heart's inordinate action, fresh air, and a properly regulated light.

Internal hemorrhage is more dangerous than external, because it is generally inaccessible. The chief remedies are copious venesection, elevated position, opium and acetate of lead, cool air and cool drinks.

Exhaustion from hemorrhage should be treated according to the principles which guide the practitioner in cases of severe shock. Opium should be given freely as soon as reaction begins to quiet the tremulous movements of the heart and tranquilize the mind. When the bleeding is internal, the reaction should be brought about gradually, not hurriedly, lest we thus become instrumental in promoting or re-exciting the hemorrhage.

Secondary hemorrhage comes on at a variable period, from a few hours to a number of days; it may depend upon imperfect ligation of the arteries, ulceration, softening or gangrene of the coats of these vessels, or upon undue constriction of the tissues by tight bandages. In some cases it is venous, and may then be owing to inadequate support of the parts. Whatever the cause may be, it should be promptly searched out, and removed.

3. The third indication is to remove all *foreign matter*. This should be done at once and effectually; with sponge and water, pressed upon the parts, with finger, or finger and forceps. Not a particle of matter, not a hair, or the smallest clot of blood must be left behind, otherwise it will be sure to provoke and keep up irritation.

4. As soon as the bleeding has been checked and the extraneous matter cleared away, the edges of the *wound* are gently and evenly

6

approximated, and permanently retained by
suture and adhesive plaster, aided, if necessary, by the bandage. The best suture,
because the least irritating, is that made
of silver wire; but if this material is not
at hand, strong, thin, well-waxed silk is
used. The adhesive strips are applied in
such a manner as to admit of free drainage.
The bandage is required chiefly in injuries
extending deeply among the muscles; when
this is the case, its use should be aided by
compresses arranged so as to force together
the deep parts of the wound.

5. When the wound is dressed, the next
duty of the surgeon is to moderate the resulting *inflammation*. For this purpose the
ordinary antiphlogistic means are employed.
In general, very little medicine will be required, except a full anodyne, as half a grain
of morphia, immediately after the patient
has sufficiently recovered from the effects of
his shock, and perhaps a mild aperient the
ensuing morning, especially if there be con-
stipation with a tendency to excessive reaction. The drinks must be cooling, and the
diet light and nutritious, or otherwise, accord-

ing to the amount of depression and loss of blood. In the latter event, a rich diet and milk-punch may be required from the beginning. A diaphoretic draught will be needed if the skin is hot and arid, aided by frequent sponging of the surface with cool or tepid water. General bleeding will rarely, if ever, be required; certainly not if the injury is at all severe, or if there has already been any considerable waste of blood and nervous fluid.

Much trouble is, at times, experienced both in civil and military practice, especially in very hot weather, in preventing the access of flies to our dressing. The larvæ which they deposit are rapidly developed into immense *maggots*, which, creeping over the wounds and sores of the patient, and gnawing the parts, cause the most horrible distress. The soldiers in Syria, under Larrey, were greatly annoyed by these insects, and our wounded in Mexico also suffered not a little from them. The best prevention is bran, or light saw-dust, with which the injured parts should be carefully covered. The use of cotton must be avoided, inasmuch as it soon becomes hot and wet—two circumstances highly favorable to incubation.

The best local applications are the water-dressings, either tepid, cool, or cold, according to the temperament of the patient, the tolerance of the parts, and the season of the year. Union by the first intention is, in all the more simple cases, the thing aimed at and steadily kept in view, and hence the less the parts are encumbered, moved or fretted, the more likely shall we be to attain the object.

The medical attendant should have a constant eye to the condition of the *bladder* after all severe injuries, of whatever character, as retention of urine is an extremely common occurrence, and should always be promptly remedied. Attention to this point is the more necessary, because the poor patient, in his comatose or insensible condition, is frequently unable to make known his wants.

Such, in a few words, are the general principles of treatment to be followed in all wounds; but there are some wounds which are characterized by peculiarities, and these peculiarities are of such practical importance

as to require separate consideration. Of this
nature are punctured, lacerated, and gunshot
wounds.

Punctured wounds are inflicted by various
kinds of weapons, as the lance, sabre, sword,
or bayonet. In civil practice they are most
generally met with as the result of injuries
inflicted by nails, needles, splinters, and fragments of bone. They often extend into the
visceral cavities, joints, vessels, and nerves;
and are liable to be followed by excessive
pain, erysipelas, and tetanus; seldom heal by
adhesive action; and often cause death by
shock or hemorrhage. When the vulnerating
body is broken off and buried, it may be difficult to find and extract it, especially when
small and deep seated. When this is the
case, the wound must be freely dilated, an eye
being had to the situation of the more important vessels and nerves. In other respects,
the general principles of treatment are similar
to those of incised wounds. Opium should
be administered largely; and, if much tension supervene, or matter form, free incisions
will be necessary.

In *lacerated wounds* the edges should be
6*

tacked together very gently, and large inter-
spaces left for drainage. A small portion
will probably unite by the first intention;
the remainder, by the granulating process.
Such wounds nearly always suppurate more
or less profusely, and some of the torn and
bruised tissues not unfrequently perish. The
same bad consequences are apt to follow them
as in punctured wounds. Warm water constitutes the best dressing, either alone or with
the addition of a little spirits of camphor.
Opium should be used freely internally, and
the diet must be supporting.

Gunshot wounds, in their general character,
partake of the nature of lacerated and contused wounds. They are, of course, the most
common and dangerous lesions met with in
military practice; often killing instantly, or,
at all events, so mutilating the patient as to
destroy him within a few hours or days after
their receipt. The most formidable wounds
of the kind are made by the conical rifle and
musket balls and by cannon balls, the latter
often carrying away the greater portion of a
limb, or mashing and pulpifying the muscles
and viscera in the most frightful and destruc-

tive manner; while the former commit terrible ravages among the bones, breaking them into numerous fragments, each of which may, in its turn, tear up the soft tissues in a way perhaps not less mischievous than the ball itself. The old round ball is a much less fatal weapon than the conical, which seldom becomes flattened, and which has been known to pass through the bodies of two men and lodge in that of a third some distance off.

When a ball lodges it makes generally only one orifice; but it should be remembered that it may make two, three, and even four, and at last bury itself more or less deeply. Such cases are, however, uncommon. Should the missile escape, there will necessarily be two openings; or, if it meet a sharp bone and be thereby divided or cut in pieces, as sometimes happens, there may be even three. The orifice of entrance and the orifice of exit differ in their appearances. The first is small, round, and often a little discolored from the explosion of the powder; the other, on the contrary, is comparatively large, slit-like, everted, and free from color. These differences, however, are frequently very trifling, particularly if the ball be projected with great velocity and it do not encounter any bone. The opening of entrance made by the round ball is often a little depressed or inverted, but such an appearance is extremely uncommon in wounds made by the conical ball.

It is often a matter of great importance to determine, when two openings exist in a limb, whether they have been made by one ball, which has passed out, or by two balls, which are retained. The question is of grave importance, both in a practical and in a medico-legal point of view; but its solution is, unfortunately, not always possible. Sometimes the openings of entrance and exit are materially modified by the introduction but non-escape of a foreign body, as a piece of breast-plate, belt, or buckle, along with the ball, which alone passes out, or by the flattening of a ball against a bone, or its division by a bone into several fragments, each of which may afterward produce a separate orifice. Generally speaking, the missile, at the place of entrance, carries away a piece of skin, and rends the skin where it escapes, the former being often found in the wound.

Bullets sometimes glance, bruising the skin, but not penetrating it; at other times they effect an entrance, but, instead of passing on in a straight line, are deflected, coursing, perhaps, partially round the head, chest, or abdomen, or round a limb. Such results are most commonly caused by a partially spent bullet coming in contact with bones, aponeuroses, and tendons; and the round is more frequently served in this way than the conical.

Gunshot wounds bleed profusely only when a tolerably large artery has been injured, and in this event they may speedily prove fatal. During the Crimean war, however, many cases occurred in which there was no immediate hemorrhage, imperiling life, notwithstanding the limbs, lower as well as upper, were left hanging merely by the integuments. Under such circumstances, *intermediary* hemorrhage, as it is termed, is apt to show itself as soon as reaction takes place—generally within a few hours after the accident.

The pain is of a dull, burning, smarting, or aching character, and the patient is pale, weak, tremulous, nauseated, and despondent, often in a degree far beyond what might be expected from the apparent violence of the injury, and that, too, perhaps, when the individual is of the most undaunted courage and self-possession in the heat of battle. At other times a man may have a limb torn off, or be injured in some vital organ, and yet hardly experience any shock whatever; nay, perhaps be scarcely conscious that he is seriously hurt. The pain and prostration are always greater, other things being equal, when a bone has been crushed or a large joint laid open, than when there is a mere flesh wound.

The gravity of gunshot wounds of the *joints* has been recognized by all practitioners, both military and civil, from time immemorial. The principal circumstances of the prognosis are the size and complexity of the articulation, the extent of the injury, and the state of the system. A gunshot wound of a ginglymoid joint is, in general, a more dangerous affair than a similar one of a ball-and-socket joint. The structures around the articulation often suffer severely, thus adding greatly to the risk of limb and life. Of 65 cases of gunshot wounds of different joints, related by Alcock, 33 recovered; but of these 21 lost the limb. Of the 32 that died no operation was performed upon 18.

Gunshot wounds of the smaller joints, even those of the ankle, often do very well, although they always require long and careful treatment. Lesions of this kind, involving the shoulder, are frequently amenable to ordinary means. If the ball lodges in the head of the humerus, it must be extracted without delay, its retention being sure to excite violent inflammation in the soft parts, and caries or necrosis in the bone, ultimately necessitating amputation, if not causing death.

Gunshot wounds of the *knee-joint* are among the most dangerous of accidents, and no attempt should be made to save the limb when the injury is at all extensive, especially if it involves fracture of the head of the tibia or condyles of the femur. Even extensive laceration of the ligament of the patella should, I think, as a general rule, be regarded as a sufficient cause of amputation. In 1854, Macleod saw upwards of forty cases of gunshot wounds of the knee in the French hospitals in the Crimea, and all, except one, in which an attempt was made to save the limb, proved fatal. Of nine cases which occurred in India not one was saved. Guthrie never saw a patient recover from a gunshot wound of the knee-joint; and Esmarch, who served in the Schleswig-Holstein wars, expressly declares that all lesions of this kind demand immediate amputation of the thigh.

When, in bad cases of these articular injuries, an attempt is made to save the limb, the patient often perishes within the first three or four days, from the conjoined effects of shock, hemorrhage, and traumatic fever. If he survives for any length of time, large abscesses are apt to form in and around the joint, the matter burrowing extensively among the muscles, and causing detachment of the periosteum with caries and necrosis of the bones.

Muscles, badly injured by bullets, generally suppurate, and are very apt to become permanently useless. Special pains should therefore be taken to counteract this tendency during the cure. Large shot and other foreign bodies sometimes lodge among these structures, where their presence may remain for a long time unsuspected.

Cannon balls often do immense mischief

by striking the surface of the body obliquely, pulpifying the soft structures, crushing the bones, lacerating the large vessels and nerves, and tearing open the joints, without, perhaps, materially injuring the skin.

A very terrible form of *contusion* is often inflicted upon the upper extremity of artillerymen by the premature explosion of the gun while in the act of loading; causing excessive commotion of the entire limb, laceration of the soft parts, and most extensive infiltration of blood, accompanied, in many cases, by comminuted fracture, and penetration of the wrist and elbow joints. The constitutional shock is frequently great. If an attempt be made to save the parts, diffusive suppuration, and more or less gangrene, will be sure to follow, bringing life into imminent jeopardy. An attempt in such a case to save the limb would be worse than useless, if, indeed, not criminal; amputation must be promptly performed, and that at a considerable distance above the apparent seat of the injury, otherwise mortification might seize upon the stump.

In the *treatment* of this class of injuries,

the first thing to be done, after arresting the
hemorrhage and relieving shock, is to extract
the ball and any other foreign substance that
may have entered along with it, the next being
to guard against inflammation and other bad
consequences.

In order to ascertain where the ball is, the
limb should be placed as nearly as possible in
the position it was supposed to have been at the
moment of the accident. A long, stout, flex-
ible, blunt-pointed probe, like that sketched
in the annexed cut, or a straight silver catheter, is then passed along the track and gently
moved about until it strikes the ball.. In
many cases the best probe is the surgeon's
finger. Valuable information may often be
obtained by the process of pinching, or digital
compression, the ends of the fingers being
firmly and regularly pressed against the
wounded structures, bones as well as muscles, tendons, and aponeuroses. Occasionally,
again, as when a ball is lodged in an extremity, its presence is easily detected by the
patient, who may make such an examination
as he lies in bed.

The situation of the foreign body having

been ascertained, the bullet-forceps, seen in the
accompanying engraving, take
the place of the probe, the
blades, which should be long
and slender, being closed until they come in contact with
the ball, when they are ex-
panded so as to grasp it, care
being taken not to include any
of the soft tissues. If there
be any loose or detached splinters of bone, wadding, or other
foreign material, it should now
also be removed; it being constantly borne in mind that,
while a ball may occasionally
become encysted, and is at
all times, if smooth, a comparatively harmless tenant,
such substances always keep
up irritation, and should,
therefore, if possible, be got
rid of without delay.

Although preference is commonly given to
the bullet-forceps, properly so called, as an
extractor, the polypus and dressing-forceps,

represented in the annexed figures, generally answer quite as well, especially the former, the latter being adapted only to cases where the foreign body is situated a short distance below the surface, or where the wound is of unusual dimensions, admitting of the free play of the instrument.

During the extraction, the parts should be properly supported, and if the wound is not large enough for the expansion of the instrument, it must be suitably enlarged. When the ball is lodged a short distance from the skin, it may often be readily reached by a counter-opening.

When a bullet is imbedded in a bone, as in the head of the tibia, or in the condyles of the femur, and the parts are not so much injured as to demand amputation, extraction may be effected with the aid of the trephine and elevator. Sometimes a bullet-worm, as it is termed, an instrument similar to that used in drawing a ball from a gun, will be very convenient for its removal.

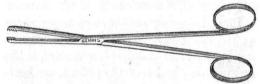

The operation being completed, the parts are placed in an easy, elevated position, and enveloped in tepid, cool or cold water-dress-ings, as may be most agreeable to them and to the system. The best plan, almost always, is to leave the opening or openings, made by the ball, free, to favor drainage and prevent pain and tension. If the track be very narrow, it may heal by the first intention, but in general it will suppurate, and portions of tissue may even mortify. Erysipelas, pyemia, and se-condary hemorrhage are some of the bad consequences after gunshot injuries, the latter usually coming on between the fifth and ninth day, the period of the separation of the sloughs.

7*

CHAPTER VI.

Amputations and Resections.

In endeavoring to decide so important a question as the loss of a limb, various circumstances are to be considered, as the age, habits and previous health of the patient, the kinds of injury, and the number, nature, and importance of the tissues involved. In military practice amputation must often be performed in cases where in civil practice it might be avoided.

It may be assumed, as a rule, that young adults bear up under severe accidents and operations, other things being equal, much better than children and elderly subjects; the strong than the feeble; the temperate than the intemperate; the residents of the country than the inhabitants of the crowded city.

The following circumstances may be enumerated as justifying, if not imperatively demanding, amputation in cases of wounds, whatever may be their nature :—

1st. When a limb has been struck by a cannon ball or run over by a railroad car, fracturing the bones, and tearing open the soft parts, amputation should, as a general rule, be performed, even when the injury done to the skin and vessels is apparently very slight, experience having shown that such accidents seldom do well, if an attempt is made to save the limb, the patient soon dying of gangrene, pyemia, or typhoid irritation. The danger of an unfavorable termination in such a case is always greater when the lesion affects the lower extremity than when it involves the superior.

2d. No attempt should be made to save a limb when, in addition to serious injury done to the integuments, muscles, or bones, its principal artery, vein, or nerve has been extensively lacerated, or violently contused, as the result will be likely to be gangrene, followed by death.

3d. A lacerated or gunshot wound penetrating a large joint, as that of the knee or ankle, and accompanied by comminuted fracture, or extensive laceration of the ligaments of the articulation, will, if left to itself, be very prone to terminate in mortification, and is therefore a proper case for early amputation.

4th. Gunshot wounds attended with severe comminution of the bones, the fragments being sent widely around among the soft parts, lacerating and bruising them severely, generally require amputation, especially in naval and military practice.

5th. Extensive laceration, contusion, and stripping off of the integuments, conjoined with fracture, dislocation, or compression and pulpification of the muscles, will, in general, be a proper cause for the removal of a limb.*

Amputation is not to be performed, in any case, until sufficient reaction has taken place to enable the patient to bear the additional shock and loss of blood. As long as he is deadly pale, the pulse small and thready, the surface cold, and the thirst, restlessness, and jactitation excessive, it is obvious that recourse to the knife must be wholly out of the question. The proper treatment is recumbency, with mild stimulants, sinapisms to the extremities, and other means calculated to re-excite the

* Gross's Surgery, vol. i. p. 395.

action of the heart and brain. Power being restored, the operation, if deemed necessary, is proceeded with, due regard being had to the prevention of shock and hemorrhage, the two things now mainly to be dreaded.

One of the great obstacles about immediate amputation is the difficulty which the surgeon so often experiences in respect to the cases demanding the operation, and the uncertainty that none of the internal organs have sustained fatal injury; a circumstance which would, of course, contra-indicate the propriety of such interference.

Cases occur, although rarely, where, notwithstanding the most violent injury, or perhaps, even the loss of a limb, there is hardly any appreciable shock, and, in such an event, the operation should be performed on the spot.

The results of the military surgery in the Crimea show that the success of amputations was very fair when performed early, but most unfortunate when they were put off for any length of time. This was the case, it would seem, both in the English and French armies.

Should amputation ever be performed in spreading gangrene? The answer to this

question must depend upon circumstances.
We may give our sanction when the disease,
although rapid, is still limited, and when the
patient, comparatively stout and robust, has
a good pulse, with no serious lesion of a vital
organ and no despair of his recovery, but a
cheerful, buoyant mind, hopeful of a favorable issue. No operation is to be done when
the reverse is the case; if it be, the patient
will either perish on the table, from shock
and hemorrhage, or from a recurrence of
mortification in the stump.

Lacerated, contused, and gunshot wounds
are often of so frightful a nature as to render
it perfectly certain, even at a glance, that the
limb will be obliged to be sacrificed in order
that a better chance may be afforded for pre-
serving the patient's life. At other times,
the injury, although severe, may yet, apparently, not be so desperate as to preclude, in
the opinion of the practitioner, the possibility
of saving the parts, or, at all events, the propriety of making an attempt to that effect.
The cases which may reasonably require and
those which may not require interference with
the knife are not always so clearly and dis-

tinctly defined as not to give rise, in very
many instances, to the most serious and un-
pleasant apprehension, lest we should be
guilty, on the one hand, of the sin of commission, and, on the other, of that of omis-
sion; or, in other and more comprehensive
terms, that, while the surgeon endeavors to
avoid Scylla, he may not unwittingly run into
Charybdis, mutilating a limb that might have
been saved, and endangering life by the retention of one that should have been promptly
amputated. It is not every man, however
large his skill and experience, that is always
able to satisfy himself, even after the most
profound deliberation, what line of conduct
should be pursued in these trying circumstances; hence the safest plan for him generally is to procure the best counsel that the
emergencies of the case may admit of. But
in doing this, he must be careful to guard
against procrastination; the case must be met
promptly and courageously; delay even of a
few hours may be fatal, or, at all events, place
limb and life in imminent jeopardy. Above
all, let proper caution be used if the patient
is obliged to be transported to some hospital,

or to a distant home, that he may not be
subjected to unnecessary pain, exposed to loss
of blood, or carried in a position incompatible
with his exhausted condition. Vast injury is
often done in this way, by ignorant persons
having charge of the case, and occasionally
even by practitioners whose education and
common sense should be a sufficient guarantee
against such conduct.

Little need be said here about the *methods*
of amputation. In cases of emergency, where
time is precious, and the number of surgeons
inadequate, the flap operation deserves, in my
opinion, a decided preference over the circular,
and, in fact, over every other. The rapidity
with which it may be executed, the abundant
covering which it affords for the bone, and the
facility with which the parts unite are qualities
which strongly recommend it to the judgment
of the military surgeon. The flaps should be
long and well shaped, and care taken to cut
off the larger nerves on a level with the bone,
in order to guard against the occurrence of
neuralgia after the wound is healed. Whatever method be adopted, a long stump should
be aimed at, that it may afford a good lever-

age for the artificial substitute. No blood
should be lost during or after the operation,
and hence the main artery of the limb should
always be thoroughly compressed by a tourniquet, not by the fingers of assistants, who are
seldom, if ever, trustworthy on such occasions.

Anæsthetics should be given only in the
event of thorough reaction; so long as the
vital powers are depressed and the mind is
bewildered by shock, or loss of blood, their
administration will hardly be safe, unless the
greatest vigilance be employed, and this is
not always possible on the field of battle, or
even in the hospital. Moreover, it is astonishing what little suffering the patient generally
experiences, when in this condition, even from
a severe wound or operation.

In the war in the Crimea, the British
used chloroform almost universally in their
operations; the French also exhibited it very
extensively, and Baudens, one of their leading
military surgical authorities, declares that they
did not meet with one fatal accident from it, although it was given by them, during the East-
ern campaign, thirty thousand times at least.
The administration of chloroform is stated

8

by Macleod to have contributed immensely to the success of primary amputations.

The *dressings* should be applied according to the principles laid down under the head of wounds. The sutures, made with silver wire or fine silk, should not be too numerous, and the adhesive strips must be so arranged as to admit of thorough drainage. A bandage should be applied from above downward, to control muscular action and afford support to the vessels; the stump rest upon a pillow covered with oil-cloth, and the water-dressing be used if there is danger of over-action. Pain and spasm are allayed by anodynes; traumatic fever, by mild diaphoretics. Copious purging is avoided; the drink is cooling; and the diet must be in strict conformity with the condition of the patient's system. The first dressings are removed about the end of the third day; after that once or even twice a day, according to the nature and quantity of the discharges, accumulation and bagging being faithfully guarded against.

The following *statistics* of amputations, both in the continuity of the limbs and of the

articulations, possess peculiar interest for the
military surgeon. They are derived chiefly
from a review which I published of Mr.
Macleod's "Notes of the Surgery in the
Crimea" in the North American Medico-
Chirurgical Review for January, 1860.

The number of cases given by Macleod is
732, with a mortality of 201. Of these, 654 were
primary, with 165 deaths, or 26·22 per cent.;
and 78 secondary, with 36 deaths, or in the
ratio of 46·1. The mortality of the greater
amputations—as those of the shoulder, arm,
and forearm, and the hip, thigh, knee, and
leg—was 39·8 per cent. for the primary operations, and 60 per cent. for the secondary.

The increase of mortality from amputations as we approach the trunk has long been
familiar to surgeons, and the results in the
Crimea have not changed our previous knowledge. Thus the ratio of mortality of amputations of the fingers was 0·5; of the forearm
and wrist, 1·8; of the arm, 22·9; of the
shoulder, 27·2; of the tarsus, 14·2; of the
ankle-joint, 22·2; of the leg, 30·3; of the
knee-joint, 50·0; and of the thigh, in its
lower third, 50·0, at its middle, 55·3, at the

upper part, 86·8, and at the hip, 100·0. The
limb was removed at the latter joint in 10
cases, all of which rapidly proved fatal. The
French had 13 cases, primary and secondary,
with no better luck.

Legouest has published a table of most of
the recorded cases of amputation at the *hip-
joint*, for gunshot wounds. Of these 30 were
primary, and all ended fatally; of 11 inter-
mediate, or early secondary, 3 recovered;
and of 3 remote, 1 recovered. "Thus," says
Macleod, "if we sum up the whole, we have
4 recoveries in 44 cases, or a mortality of
90·9 per cent." Some of the primary cases
died on the table; and all the rest, except
two, before the tenth day. In the Schleswig-
Holstein war, amputation at the hip-joint was
performed seven times, with one cure. Mr.
Sands Cox, recording the experience of civil
and military hospitals up to 1846, gives 84
cases, most of them for injury, with 26 recoveries. Dr. Stephen Smith, of New York,
has published tables of 98 cases, showing a
ratio of mortality of 1 in $2\frac{2}{3}$. In 62 of these
cases, the operation was performed in 30 for
injury, with a mortality of 60 per cent.

Amputation in the upper third of the *thigh* was performed 39 times, with a fatal result in 34. Of these cases only one was secondary, and that perished. Amputation of the middle third of the limb was performed in 65 cases, of which 38 died. Of these cases 56 were primary, with 31 deaths, giving thus a mortality of 53·3 per cent.; 9 cases were operated upon at a later period, and of these, 7 died, or 77·7 per cent. Amputation of the lower third of the thigh was performed 60 times, 46 being primary, with a mortality of 50 per cent., and 14 secondary, with a mortality of 71·4 per cent.

Amputation at the *knee* was performed primarily in 6 cases, of which 3 died, and once secondarily, with a fatal result. Chelius refers to 37 cases of amputation of the knee, collected by Jæger, of which 22 were favorable; and of 18 cases recorded by Dr. Markoe, of New York, as having occurred in the practice of American surgeons, 13 got well. These cases, added together, afford an aggregate of 61, with a mortality of 21, or 34·4 per cent.

The *leg* was amputated 101 times, with 36

8*

deaths, or a mortality of 35·6 per cent. Of these cases 89 were primary, with 28 deaths, and 12 secondary, with 8 deaths.

Amputation at the *ankle-joint* was performed in 12 cases, death following in 2. Of these cases 3 were secondary, and all favorable.

The arm was removed at the *shoulder-joint* in 39 cases, with a fatal issue in 13, or 33·3 per cent., 33 being primary, with 9 deaths, and 6 secondary, with a fatal issue in 4. If we couple these cases with 21 that occurred during the previous period of the war, we shall have an aggregate of 60 cases, with 19 deaths, or a mortality of 31·6 per cent. The advantage of primary over secondary amputation of the shoulder has long been known to military surgeons. Thus, of 19 primary cases mentioned by Mr. Guthrie as having occurred between June and September, 1813, 18 recovered, while of 19 secondary cases 15 died. The experience of the late Dr. Thomson, in Belgium, is equally decisive.

Amputation of the upper *arm* was performed 102 times, with death in 25 cases, or a mortality of 24·5; 96 of the cases being primary. Of the 6 secondary cases one-half proved fatal.

The *forearm* was amputated primarily 52 times, and the hand at the wrist once, with only 1 death; while of 7 secondary operations upon the same parts, 2 died.

Resection is one of the aids of conservative surgery, and military practice affords numerous occasions for its employment. The operation, however, is not equally applicable to all the articulations. Resection of the *shoulder-joint* has hitherto afforded the most flattering results. It is more especially applicable in cases of gunshot injuries, unattended by serious lesion of the vessels and nerves of the limb, or severe laceration of the muscles and integuments. A portion of the humerus, embracing, if necessary, from four to five inches in length, together with a part or even the whole of the glenoid cavity of the scapula, may be safely and expeditiously removed under such circumstances, and yet the patient have an excellent use of his arm.

Williams mentions 19 cases of gunshot

wounds of the shoulder-joint in which resection was performed, of which 3 proved fatal. Baudens saved 13 out of 14 cases, and the British surgeons in the Crimea lost 2 patients only out of 27.

Resection of the *elbow* has of late engaged much attention among military men, and although the results are less flattering than in the operation upon the shoulder, they are, nevertheless, highly encouraging. Of 82 cases which occurred in the Schleswig-Holstein and in the Crimean campaigns, only 16 died, or 1 in about 5.

The *wrist-joint* has seldom been the subject of excision; doubtless, cases not unfrequently occur in which it might be resorted to with advantage.

Dr. George Williams has collected the history of 11 cases of excision of the *hip-joint* for gunshot injury, 6 of which occurred in the Crimea. Of this number 10 died. Of 23 amputations at the hip-joint by the English and French surgeons in the East, all died.

Excision of the *knee-joint* for gunshot injury holds out no prospect of advantage, experience having shown that, when the ar-

ticulating extremities of the femur and tibia
are fractured by a ball, the proper remedy is
amputation.

The *ankle-joint* has been resected in a few
instances only for gunshot injuries, and the
results have thus far been by no means flattering. When the joint is seriously implicated, amputation will undoubtedly be the
more judicious procedure.

Resection of the bones in their continuity
is seldom practiced in this class of injuries,
and experience has offered nothing in its
favor. The operation was performed several
times in the Crimea, but proved invariably
fatal.

The *after-treatment* in resection must be
conducted upon the same principles as in
amputation. The measures must, for the
most part, be of a corroborating nature. The
limb must be placed in an easy position, and
be well supported by a splint or fracture-box,
to prevent motion. The operation is liable
to be followed by the same bad effects as
amputations.

CHAPTER VII.

Ill Consequences of Wounds and Operations.

THE bad consequences to be apprehended after wounds, amputations, and other operations, are traumatic fever, hemorrhage, excessive suppuration, spasm, erysipelas, gangrene, pyemia, and tetanus.

a. Traumatic fever usually sets in within the first few hours after the injury, or soon after reaction has been fairly established. In camp practice its tendency generally is to assume a low typhoid character, especially if there is much crowding of the sick, with imperfect ventilation and want of cleanliness. Not unfrequently it displays an endemic or epidemic disposition.

The treatment must be exceedingly mild; the patient will not bear depletion, but will, notwithstanding his fever, probably require stimulants and tonics, with nutritious food and drink from the very commencement. A gentle anodyne and diaphoretic mixture, as morphia and antimony in camphor-water, may be needful, in the early stage, to quell the fictitious excitement or attempt at overaction.

b. The likelihood of *secondary hemorrhage* must be steadily kept in view in these cases; much may be done to prevent it by the proper use of the ligature at the time of the operation or dressing, but it is often unavoidable, especially in gunshot wounds, owing to the injury sustained by the coats of the vessels by the grazing of the ball. However induced, it should receive the most prompt attention, inasmuch as the loss even of a few ounces of blood may prove destructive to the already exhausted system.

c. Spasm of the muscles is not peculiar to amputations; it often exists in a most severe degree in cases of fractures and gunshot wounds. Anodynes in full doses, with a little antimony, the use of a moderately-tight bandage, and warm water-dressing, medicated with laudanum and acetate of lead, are the most appropriate measures.

d. Profuse suppuration may be looked for in nearly all bad wounds, whatever their character, and also in many of the amputations performed on the field of battle. The exhausting effects must be counteracted by supporting remedies, as quinine, iron, cod-liver oil, and brandy, with frequent change of dressing, cleanliness, and ventilation. Bagging is prevented by counter-openings and careful bandaging.

e. *Erysipelas* usually manifests itself within the first thirty-six hours after the injury or operation; often assumes an endemic or epidemic character; is easily distinguished by the peculiar reddish blush rapidly spreading over the surface, together with the stinging or smarting pain and increased swelling; and should be treated with dilute tincture of iodine, or anodyne and saturnine lotions, quinine and tincture of iron, with nutritious food and drinks.

f. *Gangrene* is sufficiently common after severe lesions on the battle-field, especially that variety of it denominated hospital gangrene. During the Crimean war, this form of gangrene raged with extraordinary virulence and fatality among the French in the hospitals on the Bosphorus. It also prevailed

about the same period within some of the hospitals in the south of France, and it is asserted that the "Euphrate," a transport
ship, in her voyage to the Mediterranean was
obliged, from this cause alone, to throw sixty
of her men overboard within thirty-six hours!
After the taking of the Quarries and the as-
sault upon the Redan, during the heat of
summer, in 1855, the English surgeons lost
a number of their cases of amputation of the
thigh from moist gangrene of a most rapid
character, the system having been literally
everwhelmed by the poison. When hospital
gangrene is endemic, it attacks not only open
wounds and sores, but also the slightest
scratches, cicatrices, and stumps. Persons
laboring under diarrhœa, dysentery, and
scurvy are most obnoxious to it.

The proper remedies are sequestration of
the patients, the free use of the nitric acid lotion, iodine to the inflamed skin, charcoal, port
wine, or yeast cataplasms, and frequent ablutions with disinfecting fluids, aided by opium,
quinine, tincture of iron, lemon-juice, and
other supporting means. Mopping the af-
9

fected surface freely with strong nitric acid often answers an excellent purpose. The favorite remedy of Pouteau was the actual cautery.

g. Pyemia, the purulent infection of the French writers, is one of the chief dangers after severe wounds and operations. It was the great source of the mortality after amputations, especially secondary, during the war in the Crimea. It usually comes on within from three to eight days after the injury, and is nearly always fatal. Its characteristic symptoms are rigors, followed by copious sweats, rapid failure of the vital powers, delirium, and a withered appearance of the countenance, frequently conjoined with an icterode tinge of the eye and skin. On dissection, the large veins leading from the stump or wound are found filled with pus, with redness of the lining membrane; and abscesses, usually small and filled with unhealthy fluid, are seen scattered through the lungs, muscles, and cellular substance, matter also occasionally existing in the joints. The treatment is essentially the same as in erysipelas.

h. Traumatic tetanus is not very common in military practice. It is most liable to show itself in tropical countries, in hot, damp weather, and in persons of a nervous, irritable temperament, occasionally supervening upon the most insignificant injuries, as, for example, a mere scratch. In India the disease is often provoked by unextracted balls, and both in that country and on the continent of Europe the operation which was most frequently followed by it, during the recent wars, was amputation at the shoulder-joint.

The effects of sudden vicissitudes of temperature in developing tetanus, are well known. They are most striking in tropical regions, when the change is from hot to cold, or from dry to wet. Larrey had repeated opportunities of observing the development of the disease under such circumstances, both in Egypt and Germany. After the battle of Bautzen, the exposure of the wounded to the cold night air produced over a hundred cases of tetanus, and a large number suffered from a similar cause after the battle of Dresden. Like effects were witnessed at Ferozepore and Chillianwallah. Baudens, in his treatise

on gunshot wounds, states that the influence
of cold and moisture in developing the disease,
during the French campaigns in Africa, was
most striking. Of forty slightly wounded
men, placed in a gallery on the ground floor,
during the prevalence of a northeasterly
wind, fifteen were speedily attacked with
tetanus. Similar effects have several times
been noticed in this country. Thus, after
the battle of Ticonderoga, in 1758, nine of
the wounded who were exposed the whole
night after the action, in open boats upon
Lake George, died of locked-jaw; and during
our war with Great Britain, most of those
who suffered on board the Amazon, in the
engagement before Charleston, were attacked ·
with this disease a fortnight after, in consequence of a very sudden change of weather,
the wind blowing cold and wet.

The extremes of heat and cold both favor
the production of tetanus. In the East and
West Indies, the slightest prick of the finger
or toe is often sufficient to induce the disease,
and the inhabitants of the Arctic regions not
unfrequently suffer in a similar manner. Dr.
Kane, in his memorable expedition, lost two

of his men from this affection, and he adds
that all his dogs perished from a like cause.

The *mortality* from traumatic tetanus is
notorious.　Hardly one recovers.　Nearly
all perish in two or three days from the
attack.

The most reliable remedies are opium,
in the form of morphia or acetated tincture, in large doses, in union with camphor
and antimony.　The effects of Indian hemp
are uncertain.　Chloroform will mitigate pain
and spasm.　Amputation, except, perhaps,
when the wound affects a finger or toe, will be
worse than useless, as will also be counter-irri-
tation along the spine.　To prevent the disease
should be our business, and to do this no
wounded person should ever be exposed to
the cold night air, or to currents of air at
any time.　*After all amputations, however
trifling, special directions should be given
upon this point.*

9*

CHAPTER VIII.

Injuries of the Head, Chest, and Abdomen.

THE immediate effects of *concussion* of the brain are those of fainting or collapse, and must be treated accordingly; by recumbency, access of cold air, the use of the fan, dashing of cold water upon the face and chest, and sinapisms to the precordial region, thighs, feet, and spine, aided, in the more severe cases, by stimulating injections. If the patient can swallow, he may take a little wine or brandy. A smelling-bottle may be held near, not to, the nose. Reaction is not promoted too rapidly, for fear of secondary consequences.

The period of danger from collapse being over, the patient is sedulously watched, that overaction may not occur, the risk now being from inflammation; or, the stage of excitement being happily passed, from the remote effects of the injury. If the concussion was

at all severe, all bodily and mental excitement must be for a long time avoided.

Compression of the brain arises, surgically
speaking, from two causes only: effusion of
blood, and depressed bone. In the former
case, the characteristic symptoms — insensi-
bility and coma, dilated and fixed pupil,
stertorous breathing, and paralysis — frequently do not come until some time after
the receipt of the injury. The first symptoms will probably be those of concussion, or
exhaustion. By-and-by, the patient regains
his senses and his strength, gets up, talks,
or walks, and then suddenly drops down, as
if he had been shot, in a state of utter unconsciousness. The effusion of blood, kept in
abeyance during the collapse, has had full
play, filling empty places, and causing unmis-
takable effects. Such an occurrence will be
most apt to happen when there has been extensive separation of the dura mater, or rup-
ture of the middle meningeal artery. If, on
the other hand, the compression is due to depression of the skull, the symptoms are nearly
always immediate.

When the case is one of sanguineous compression, it must be treated very much as one of ordinary apoplexy; at first, by efforts at *gradual* reaction, and afterward by purgatives, bleeding, and means to favor cerebral accommodation and prevent inflammation. The trephine is not thought of unless the unconsciousness obstinately persists, and there is reason to believe, from the nature of the phenomena, especially the existence of a wound or contusion on the head, that the blood may be reached by the instrument.

Gunshot injuries of the skull, with or without lodgment of the ball, may be productive merely of concussion of the brain, or of concussion and compression. When the missile penetrates the bone, and tears up the cerebral tissues and membranes, death usually occurs instantly, or within a short time after the receipt of the accident, without, perhaps, any attempt at reaction. Nevertheless, a number of cases of injury of this nature, in which the patient either partially or completely recovered, have been recorded by military surgeons. In some instances the ball merely penetrates the skull, with no

apparent depression, and in this event the
treatment should evidently be very simple,
being limited, in great degree, after the occurrence of reaction, to the prevention of inflammation of the brain. A similar course should
be adopted when the bone is broken and only
slightly depressed, especially if there be no
urgent or obstinate symptoms of compression.
When, on the contrary, the bone is badly
fractured, comminuted, or forced greatly
beyond the natural level, the proper plan is
to trephine, whether there be any external
wound or evidences of compression or not.
If the operation be neglected, loss of life
from inflammation will be sure to arise within
the first six or ten days after the receipt of
the injury. In the punctured fracture, as it
is named, the trephine is invariably employed
at the earliest moment, however flattering,
apparently, the head symptoms may be. If
the instrument be withheld, fatal cerebritis or
arachnitis will be no less certain than when
the bone is shattered and driven down upon
the brain.

Fracture of the skull by *contre-coup*, so
common in civil practice, is seldom met with

on the field of battle; doubtless for the reason that the injury is hardly ever inflicted
upon the top or base of the cranium, as it is
when a person is struck upon the vertex or
falls upon his nates. The most frequent
fracture among soldiers is the punctured. A
ball has been known to break the internal
table of the skull without the external.

The skull is sometimes frightfully injured
without any serious lesion of the scalp.
Macleod refers to a case, which occurred at
the Alma, where it was completely destroyed
by a glancing shot, without any material
implication of the soft parts. A round shot
(" en ricochet ") struck the scale from an
officer's shoulder, and merely grazed his head
as it ascended. The result was instant death.
The skull was so completely mashed that
its fragments rattled under the scalp as if
loose in a bag. The condition of the brain
was, unfortunately, not ascertained.

In the more simple forms of fractures of
the skull, however induced, the practice of
trephining is now much less common than
formerly, and there is no doubt that the
patient often makes a good recovery, though

it is by no means certain that such a person
may not suffer seriously, at a more or less
remote period, from epileptic and other
affections. I am convinced from my own
observation that this happens not unfrequently. Dr. Stromeyer, surgeon-in-chief in
the Schleswig-Holstein campaign in 1849,
expresses strong opposition to the use of
the trephine in gunshot and other fractures
of the skull, even with depression, on the
ground that, independently of the mischief
inflicted in the operation upon the tissues,
admission of air to the contused portion of
the brain greatly augments the danger of
inflammation. Of 41 cases of gunshot fractures of the skull with depression, reported
by him, 34 were cured, and of these 1 only
had been trephined.

When operative interference is deemed im-
proper, the most simple treatment should be
enforced. Any probing that may be necessary should, if practicable, be performed with
the finger, and the wound should not be enlarged, except when we are compelled to ele-
vate depressed or remove loose bone.

When trephining is required, it should be

done as early as possible, and without chloroform or ether, unless the patient is very un-
ruly, as the anæsthetic might tend to provoke
inflammation of the brain. Every particle of
depressed bone should be elevated, and such
portions as are loose, detached, or driven into
the brain, and easily accessible, removed. All
bleeding vessels are tied, the edges of the
wound are *gently* approximated with silver
sutures, and the head, well shaved and raised,
wrapped in warm or cold water-dressing, as
may be most grateful to part and system.
The great danger after all severe injuries and
operations upon the skull is inflammation of
the brain and of its membranes, and to the
prevention of this, therefore, the surgeon
should direct his most zealous efforts. The
patient must be frequently visited, and every
untoward symptom promptly met by appropriate measures, of which active purgation,
loss of blood by venesection, leeching or cup-
ping, a restricted diet, and exclusion of light
and noise from the apartment, with perfect
rest, are the most reliable.

Wounds of the *brain* must be managed
upon general principles; all foreign matter is

at once removed, and the parts being restored as nearly as may be to their normal relations, the surgeon endeavors to keep the resulting inflammation within proper limits. Most of such lesions prove fatal within the first week from their receipt. If the patient survive for any length of time, death will generally come at last from exhaustion, cerebritis, or fungus.

Portions of the *skull*, sliced off by the sabre or sword, should be immediately replaced and secured by wire sutures, even if they are attached merely by small shreds of the scalp.

Scalp wounds of every description, but in particular the contused, lacerated, punctured, and gunshot, are extremely prone to be followed by erysipelas; death may also occur from cerebritis, arachnitis, and pyemia. The slightest lesion, then, of this region of the body should be zealously watched.

Wounds of the *face* must be treated with an eye to the avoidance of disfiguring scars, by wire sutures and cold water-dressing. When a large portion of the lower jaw is shot away, the tongue will be apt to fall back upon the glottis, causing suffocation. The organ should

10

be drawn forward with the finger or tenacu-
lum, and the patient observe the prone position until the tendency is lost.

One of the great sources of annoyance and
danger, in gunshot wounds of the face, is
secondary hemorrhage. It frequently appears soon after the accident, and, although
it often ceases spontaneously, it is sometimes
controlled with much difficulty. Paralysis,
partial or complete, is not uncommon, owing
to injury of the branches of the facial nerve.

In the management of wounds about the
mouth, throat, and face, great care must be
taken not to allow the offensive mucous and
salivary secretions to pass into the stomach.
The neglect of this precaution is apt to be
followed by a low typhoid state of the system, very similar to what occurs in pyemia,
or blood poisoning. I have repeatedly witnessed these effects after operations upon the
jaws, mouth, and even the nose.

In fractures of the bones of the face from
gunshot an exception should be made to the
general rule of removing fragments which are
nearly detached, observation having shown,
says Mr. Macleod, that the large supply of

blood in this region will enable them to resume their connection with the other tissues,
in a way that would be fatal to similarly
placed portions in other situations.

Gunshot and other wounds of the *chest* are,
as stated elsewhere, extremely fatal; death, if
the lesion be at all severe, being usually
speedily caused by shock, hemorrhage, or as-
phyxia; or, at a more or less remote period,
by inflammation and effusion. When the lungs
are wounded, the characteristic symptoms will
be hæmoptysis, with suffocative cough, great
prostration, and excessive alarm. A copious
flow of blood may take place in the thoracic
cavity from a wound of one of the intercostal
arteries.

Any foreign matter that is easily accessible
is at once removed, but officious probing is out
of the question. The wound, if small and
unaccompanied by serious hemorrhage, is
closed in the usual manner, the chest being
firmly encircled by a broad bandage, to com-
pel diaphragmatic respiration. Under opposite circumstances, it is kept open, the patient lying upon the affected side to favor the
escape of blood, with as much elevation of

the head as the case may admit of. The main
reliance for arresting pulmonary bleeding is
upon venesection, copious, and frequently repeated, unless the exhaustion amounts to absolute collapse. Sugar of lead, opium, and veratrum viride are frequently exhibited, sinapisms
are applied to the extremities, and, in short,
everything is done to control cardiac action.
Inflammatory symptoms are counteracted in
the usual manner, and effused fluids, causing
oppression, and resisting ordinary measures,
are, unhesitatingly, evacuated by puncture,
as the only chance of escape.

Wounds of the *heart* and *aorta*, of whatever
nature, are usually fatal; now and then, however, an astonishing exception occurs.

Wounds of the *abdomen*, merely penetrating
its walls, but not its contents, are brought together by sutures extending down nearly to
the peritoneum, otherwise they will be followed by hernia. When they involve the
intestine, and are incised, they are sewed up
with a fine needle and silk thread, either in-
terruptedly or continuously, the ends of the
ligature being cut off close.

Contusions of the walls of the abdomen by

round shot are among the most dangerous injuries to which the body is exposed, often
rupturing both the hollow and solid viscera,
and rapidly causing death, without much apparent sign of so severe an accident. The
most important symptoms of these contusions
are vomiting, and pain in the abdomen; and
the great object of the treatment, in the event
the patient survives their immediate effects,
is the prevention of peritonitis, which often
comes on in the most stealthy manner. Laceration of an internal organ is nearly always
promptly fatal. Shell wounds of the walls of
the abdomen are generally followed by extensive sloughing. Abscesses among the muscles
of the abdomen are not uncommon after gunshot injuries.

Balls often traverse the walls of the abdomen for a considerable distance without en-
tering its cavity, or they pass in without injuring any of the contained viscera.

"The fatality of penetrating wounds of the
belly," observes Macleod, "will depend much
on the point of their infliction. Balls enter-
ing the liver, kidneys, or spleen are well
known to be usually mortal, although excep-

tional cases are not rare. Wounds of the
great gut are also always recognized as much
less formidable than those which implicate the
small. Thomson saw only two cases of wounds
of the small gut, after Waterloo, in the way
of recovery; but Larrey reports several.
Gunshot wounds of the stomach are also exceedingly fatal. Baudens records a remark-
able case of recovery, although complicated
with severe head injuries. The syncope which
followed the severe hemorrhage in this case
lasted for ten hours, and doubtless assisted,
along with the empty state of the stomach at
the moment of injury, in preventing a fatal
issue."

Gunshot wounds of the *bladder* occasionally
occur; the ball may penetrate the organ in
any direction, and at the same time commit
extensive havoc in the neighboring parts, both
soft and osseous. Such lesions are generally
fatal. Simple gunshot wounds, on the contrary, are sometimes recovered from, especially when they are treated by the retention
of the catheter, thus allowing the urine to flow
off as fast as it descends from the kidneys.
The operation of laying open the wounded

viscus through the perineum, as originally proposed by Dr. Walker, of Massachusetts, might
be performed in such a contingency. Such a
procedure would be much more likely to prevent urinary infiltration than the catheter,
however carefully retained, during the detachment of the sloughs, as well as before the
contiguous structures have been glazed with
lymph.

Balls, pieces of cloth, fragments of bone,
and other foreign bodies, if retained in the
bladder, generally serve as nuclei of calculi,
and should, therefore, be as speedily extracted
as possible, either through the perineum, or
by means of the forceps or lithotriptor. Quite
a number of cases, in which the operation of
lithotomy was successfully performed for the
purpose of effecting the riddance of balls
and other extraneous substances, have been
reported by different writers, as Morand,
Larrey, Baudens, Langenbeck, Guthrie, and
Hutin.

CHAPTER IX.

Diseases Incident to Troops.

THE diseases which attend armies, or molest soldiers in camps, garrisons, and hospitals, and which so often decimate their ranks, and even, at times, almost annihilate whole regiments, are the different kinds of fevers, especially typhus and typhoid, dysentery, diarrhœa, and scurvy. These are, emphatically, the enemies of military life, doing infinitely more execution than all the weapons of war, however adroitly or efficiently wielded, put together. Pneumonia, pleurisy, and hepatitis, of course, slay their thousands, and various epidemics, especially cholera, not unfrequently commit the most frightful ravages. "War," says Johnson, "has means of destruction more formidable than the cannon and the sword. Of the thousands and tens of thousands that have perished, how small a proportion ever felt the stroke of an enemy!" Frederick the Great used to say that fever cost him more men than seven pitched battles, and it has long been a matter of history that more campaigns are decided by sickness than by the sword. The great mortality which attended our armies in Mexico was occasioned, not by wounds received in battle, but by the diseases incident to men carrying on their military operations in an inhospitable climate, badly fed, subjected to fatiguing marches, and obliged to use unwholsome water. Thousands perished, during their absence, from fever, dysentery, and diarrhœa, and a still greater number from the effects of these diseases, after the return of the troops to their native soil. The latter affection, in particular, pursued many, like a relentless foe, to their graves long after they had been cheered by the sight of their homes and friends.

In the war in the Crimea disease destroyed incomparably more soldiers than the sword, the musket, and the cannon. Typhus and typhoid fever, dysentery, diarrhœa, scurvy, and, lastly, malignant cholera, annihilated vast numbers, both in the British, French, and Russian ranks. According to Dr. Macleod, whose "Notes on the Surgery of the War in

the Crimea," are so well known to the profession, the proportion of those lost among
the British by sickness to those lost by gunshot and other injuries, was, during the entire
campaign, as 16,211 to 1761, exclusive of
those killed in action. The difference he sup-
poses to have been still greater among the
French and Russian forces. In December,
1854, and in January, 1855, not less than
14,000 French soldiers were admitted into
the Crimean ambulances on account of disease, whereas, during the same period, only
1500 were admitted on account of wounds.
Of the whole number nearly 2000 died.
During the last six months of the campaign,
in which the city was stormed and taken, the
French had 21,957 wounded as an offset
against 101,128 cases of disease.*   At Wal-
cheren, in 1809, the British lost one-third of
their troops by disease, and only 16 per cent.
by wounds.   In the Peninsular war, from
January, 1811, to May, 1814, out of an ef-
fective force of 61,500 men, only 42·4 per
1000, says Macleod, were lost by wounds,
while 118·6 were lost by disease.

---

* Macleod, op. cit., 67.

The number of sick that may be expected
to be constantly on hand during any given
campaign is estimated, on an average, at 10
per cent.; but this proportion must necessarily be exceeded, especially in an invading
army, with raw, undisciplined, and unaccli-
mated troops. This was eminently true even
in the Crimea, in a climate comparatively
healthy, within a few miles of the sea. We
may well imagine what would be the effects
of the climate of the South upon the North-
ern troops, if they were to pass far, during the
hot season, beyond Mason and Dixon's line.
Disease, in its worst form, would be sure to in-
vade and thin their ranks at every step. Fever
—typhoid, typhous, remittent, intermittent,
and yellow — dysentery, diarrhœa, scurvy,
pneumonia, and inflammation of the liver
would accomplish more, infinitely more, for
the Southern cause than all the weapons of
war that could be placed in the hands of the
Southern people. Typhoid, typhus, and yellow fever, dysentery, diarrhœa, and scurvy
would, in all human probability, soon become
epidemic, and occasion a mortality truly ap-
palling. The Southern soldier, on the con-

trary, thoroughly acclimated as he is, would suffer comparatively little.

The British in the Crimean war lost 5910 men from diarrhœa and dysentery, the whole number of cases having been 52,442, affording thus a mortality of 11·26 per cent. Cholera, of which there were 7575 cases altogether, destroyed 4513, or in the ratio of 59·57 per cent. Typhus fever killed 285 out of 828 cases; fever, not typhus, 3161, out of 30,376. The French and Russian troops suffered in still larger numbers from these diseases. Macleod asserts that the former lost their men by typhus fever by thousands, and the latter by tens of thousands. The British suffered but little from intermittent fever, whereas this disease did great mischief among the French, causing serious mortality, either directly or indirectly, besides disqualifying large numbers for service.

Scurvy was another dreadful enemy which the British and French troops were compelled to encounter in the Crimea. It prevailed more or less extensively for a long time, and served to impart its livery to the other diseases of the soldiery, masking their char-

acter, and remarkably augmenting their viru-
lency.

Considering, then, the frequency of the
occurrence of these diseases, and their excessive fatality, it behooves the military surgeon
to use every means in his power to guard, in
the first place, against their outbreak, by the
employment of proper hygienic or sanitary
measures, and, in the next, to treat them with
all possible diligence and judgment when their
development is unavoidable. It is, of course,
impossible, in a work of this description, to
enter into any details upon the subject; but
there are several points which cannot, I con-
ceive, be too forcibly impressed upon the
mind of the military practitioner. I refer to
the great, the paramount importance of—
1st, proper isolation of the sick, or, what is
the same thing, the importance of not crowding them together; 2dly, free ventilation;
3dly, bodily cleanliness; 4thly, little medicine; 5thly, a good supply of fresh vegetables and fruits, especially oranges and lemons;
6thly, careful and tender nursing.

Painful experience has shown, in all parts
of the world, that the crowding together of

11

the sick and wounded is one of the worst
calamities that can befall them. For want
of this precaution, diseases, otherwise easily
manageable, often assume an epidemic character, or, in the absence of this character,
often baffle the best directed efforts for their
relief. When the wounded are crowded together they frequently become the victims of
erysipelas, hospital gangrene, pyemia, and
phlebitis; occurrences which, under better
regulations, might in many cases be entirely
prevented.

Of the propriety of constant and thorough
ventilation, it is unnecessary to speak. If
pure air is so essential in health, it is easy
enough to see how important it must be in
sickness.

Cleanliness of body should be regarded as
a religious duty; it may be effected with the
sponge and tepid, cool or cold water, according to the exigencies of the case, and cannot
be performed too frequently or too thoroughly,
care being, of course, taken not to worry or
fatigue the patient. In some instances the
water may be medicated with common salt,
potassa, vinegar, or Labarraque's solution.

Nothing is generally more grateful to the
sufferer, in the different kinds of fevers, than
frequent sponging of the surface with cool or
tepid water.

The use of heroic *medicines*, or of any
medicines in large doses, in these diseases,
and also in cases of severe wounds, cannot be
too severely reprobated. More men, there is
reason to believe, have been killed in this
manner in the armies and navies of the
world than by the sword and the cannon.
Let medicines, then, be administered sparingly. *Let the secretions be well seen to;
but purge little, and use depressants with all
possible wariness.* Give iced water, but not
too freely, and lumps of ice when there is
much thirst with gastric irritability and excessive restlessness. Mild diaphoretics and anodynes will, as a general rule, be highly efficacious, but the latter should be exhibited with
great caution when there is cerebral oppression. Lemon-juice and potassa are indispensable in scurvy, or where there is a marked
tendency to scorbutic disease. Quinine is one
of the great remedies in most, if not in all, of
these diseases, especially when, as is so often

the case, they are associated with a malarious origin. The good average dose is from two to five grains, repeated from three to five times in the twenty-four hours. When marked debility prevails, the best stimulants are brandy, in the form of milk-punch or toddy, and Madeira, Port, or Sherry wine.

Immense suffering and loss of life are often occasioned for the want of fresh vegetables and fruits in military operations, as well as in the garrison and the hospital. A daily supply of these articles should, therefore, be provided at almost any hazard and expense. In all low states of the system, however induced, the strength can never be rapidly brought up without a diet which partakes more or less of this character.

There is a form of *dysentery*, very common in India, which is exceedingly apt, when large masses of troops are habitually congregated together, to assume an epidemic character; and it is for this reason that it has often been supposed to be contagious. For such an opinion, however, there does not seem to be any valid reason. Ballingall, who witnessed at least 2000 cases of this disease,

asserts that he never once met with a circumstance tending to create such a suspicion; and
the views advanced by this eminent surgeon
are those now pretty generally, if not universally, entertained by the British practitioners in India.

"The remote causes of dysentery in India
are conceived to be heat, particularly when
combined with moisture; the immediate and
indiscriminate use of fruits; the abuse of spirituous liquors, and exposure to currents of wind
and to noxious night-dews." Troops recently
arrived from Europe are particularly prone
to the disease.

Tropical dysentery presents itself in two
varieties of form, the *acute* and the *chronic*.
The first, which is an extremely fatal disease,
is seated in the rectum and colon, the latter
being often involved through nearly its entire extent, and it frequently commits very
serious, if not irreparable, mischief in these
structures before the patient and the attendant are aware of its true character, owing to
the absence of urgent pain and pyrexia.   In
general the attack is ushered in by the ordinary symptoms of diarrhœa, such as griping

11*

pain in the bowels and frequent calls to stool
with excessive straining, the evacuations
being, at first, thin and copious but without
fetor and but little streaked with blood.
The tongue, skin, and pulse are nearly, perhaps entirely, normal. Gradually the pain
becomes more violent, as well as more fixed,
and is felt in both iliac regions, or even along
the whole track of the colon; the discharges
consist chiefly of blood and mucus, or of a
fluid resembling water in which fresh beef
has been macerated; the tongue is covered
with a white coat; the skin is either hot and
dry, or bathed with clammy perspiration;
and the straining is so excessive as to occasion prolapsus of the rectum. The pulse is,
even at this stage, often but little affected,
being, perhaps, only somewhat increased in
quickness. Sometimes, however, it is very
full, bounding, and vibratory, without much
velocity, and when this is the case it always, according to Ballingall, forebodes evil.
Toward the close of the attack, the passages
are frequently involuntary and intolerably
fetid, gangrenous portions of the mucous
coat of the bowel are sometimes extruded,

and the surface of the body emits a peculiar cadaverous smell. The average period at which death occurs is about one week, but many cases linger on much longer.

The remedies upon which the India practitioners mainly rely in the treatment of this horrible form of dysentery are venesection, mercury, and opium, leeches, purgatives, diaphoretics, warm bathing, blisters, and enemata being employed as auxiliaries. Venesection is always practiced early, and, even when the patient is not very robust, boldly, it being, apparently, regarded as the sheet anchor of the physician's hope. Calomel is administered in doses of from ten to twenty grains, along with two or three grains of opium, twice or thrice in the twenty-four hours; and, while profuse salivation is discountenanced, production of slight ptyalism is generally aimed at.

Such treatment as this seems altogether frightful to the modern American practitioner; it strikes him as unnecessarily harsh, and as well calculated to augment the mortality of the disease. We might, in this country, perhaps bleed, and that pretty freely, at the very commencement of an attack of dysentery; at all events, leech very copiously, but we would certainly draw blood sparingly if the attack had already made serious constitutional inroads, or if it was of an epidemic character; and, as to giving mercury with a view to ptyalism, however slight, few men would, I presume, be so fool-hardy. The India practitioners do not, it appears, employ quinine in the treatment of this form of dysentery; a remedy so extremely needful in many cases of this disease as it prevails in this country, especially in our Southern latitudes, where it is not unfrequently of a malarious origin.

The *chronic* form of India dysentery, termed hepatic flux, more frequently attacks persons who have been for some time inured to the climate of that country, and is always associated with biliary derangement. "This flux, like the other, often assumes at its commencement the appearance of a common diarrhœa, and becomes afterward characterized by frequent and severe fits of griping, resembling colic pains, particularly urgent about the umbilical region. Each attack of griping is generally succeeded by a call to stool, and

the evacuations are always unnatural in color
and consistence, free from any admixture of
blood, but generally of a yeasty or frothy appearance, and accompanied with large discharges of flatus; while in passing they are
attended with a sense of scalding about the
anus. The patient, after each evacuation,
feels considerably relieved, and hopes to enjoy
an interval of ease, but the recurrence of the
griping, accompanied with a sensation of air
passing through the bowels, and succeeded
again by a call to stool, give him little
respite. From the commencement of the
attack, the patient complains of nausea, want
of relish for his food, and preternatural thirst,
attended often with a disagreeable taste in the
mouth. The tongue is furred or loaded, and
not unfrequently covered with a yellow bilious
coat. The pulse is quickened and the skin
parched."*

Cholera morbus must, necessarily, in this
country, especially in our Southern latitudes,
and during the hot summer months, be a more
or less frequent attendant upon camp life,
although much may be done, by a proper ob-

* Ballingall's Military Surgery, p. 511, 1844.

servance of hygienic laws, to prevent it.
When the disease breaks out it cannot be
arrested too speedily. The most appropriate
remedies, particularly in its earlier stages,
are perfect quietude, abstinence from drink,
sinapisms to the epigastrium, and an efficient
dose of morphia and camphor, or even morphia alone. If torpor of the liver exist, blue
mass or a few grains of calomel may be advantageously combined with the anodyne.
The swallowing of small lumps of ice will
greatly assist in allaying the gastric irritability. A mustard and salt emetic will be indicated if the stomach is loaded with ingesta.
The bowels are quieted with an anodyne
enema; and, to relieve thirst and reduce heat
of skin, the surface is frequently sponged
with cool or tepid water. A combination of
carbonate of potassa and acetated tincture of
opium, with fresh lemon-juice, in peppermint
or camphor water, will often act like a charm
in relieving the gastric and intestinal irritability, the cramps, and other distressing
symptoms.

The exposure of the soldier, both in the
tent and on the field, renders him extremely
prone to *rheumatism*, frequently attended

with high inflammatory excitement and severe pain. Such an attack is often effectually put to flight if, at its inception, it be treated with a large anodyne and diaphoretic mixture, as fifteen grains of Dover's powder, a third to half a grain of sulphate of morphia with a fourth of a grain of tartar emetic, or, what is perhaps still better, a drachm of the wine of colchicum in union with a full dose of morphia or black drop. When the disease has already made some progress, an active purgative should precede the exhibition of these medicines.

Sore throat, tonsillitis, and catarrhal affections, or, what in common language are called *colds*, are very common among soldiers, especially the raw troops just mustered into service, ill clothed, inexperienced, and unaccustomed to camp life. The moment such disease sets in, no matter how light it may be, the person should be compelled to report himself at the surgeon's quarters, in order that he may receive the necessary attention and advice. Generally an attack of this kind will promptly yield to a trifling prescription, as a little hot drink, a mild aperient, or, better still, a quarter of a grain of morphia, a grain of opium, or a large dose of Dover's powder.

In an army not under strict discipline, or where proper care is not observed in enlisting, *mania à potu* is very apt to show itself, much to the annoyance of the nurses and the physicians. If, in such a case, the patient be not well secured, he may, in his perverted military ardor, do serious mischief to himself and to his attendants. A moderately active mercurial purge at the outset of the disease will often go far in quieting the system and in abridging the attack. After the medicine has operated, a mild opiate and sedative treatment will generally be the most soothing. Alcoholic stimulants are, in general, to be withheld.

Nostalgia is another complaint liable to assail the soldier, even the hardiest, especially if he is a person of strong domestic attachments, or engaged in an "affaire du cœur." It is most apt to show itself in soldiers enlisting for the foreign service, or in those who are forcibly expatriated, and is often attended with great suffering, terminating in confirmed melancholy. It is characterized by a love of

solitude, a vacant, stultified expression of the
countenance, a morose, peevish disposition,
absence of mind, pallor of the cheeks; and
progressive emaciation. Many of Bonaparte's
troops, during the campaign in Egypt, suffered from this complaint; some in a very
distressing degree. In this country, nostalgia will not be likely to occur, at least not to
any extent, as our people are essentially of a
roving habit, and of an eminently social disposition. The treatment is rather moral than
medical; agreeable amusements, kindness,
gentle but incessant occupation, and the pro-
mise of an early return to home and friends
constituting the most important means of
relief.

It is impossible, even under the most rigid
discipline, to prevent *gonorrhœa* among soldiers. They will expose themselves, in spite
of all that can be done to prevent it, and
they often pay a heavy penalty for their indulgence, not only from the suffering entailed
by the primary disease, but its different com-
plications, especially chordee, cystitis, and
orchitis. The symptoms of gonorrhœa are
too well understood to require enumeration

here. The treatment should, from the start, be rigidly antiphlogistic; by rest, low diet, active purgation, and the antimonial and saline mixture, with the addition of a small quantity of copaiba. The penis and scrotum are well supported, and covered with warm water-dressing, the former organ being bathed in tepid salt water, at least thrice daily, for twenty minutes at a time. When the discharge is greatly lessened, but not till then, recourse is had to injections of lead, sulphate of zinc, or nitrate of silver, at first very mild and gradually increased in strength, repeated every six, eight or twelve hours. The treatment is continued, in a modified form, for about five days after all the specific symptoms have vanished.

Chordee is best relieved by a full anodyne, as half a grain of morphia, in union with the fourth of a grain of tartar emetic, given toward bedtime; or by a large enema of laudanum, with warm water-dressings to the genitals.

For the relief of *cystitis* the most appropriate remedies are anodyne diaphoretics, in the form of Dover's powder, or a solution of

morphia and tartar emetic, aided by the free
use of bicarbonate of soda and moderate
quantities of diluents.

Orchitis is treated by suspension of the
affected organ, with strong lead and anodyne
lotions, and the judicious exhibition of antimony, in union with morphia or black drop.

Chancres must be thoroughly cauterized at
the beginning, either with nitrate of silver,
nitric acid, or acid nitrate of mercury; and
subsequently, or after the disease has made
some progress, like any common sore, with
mild measures; mercury being studiously
withheld, except in the hard form of the disease,
but not even then while there is much inflammation or inordinate constitutional excitement. In a word, all harsh measures must
be avoided. The patient will generally do a
thousand times better without than with
mercury. The greatest possible attention
must be paid to cleanliness, and for this purpose the parts should be frequently bathed in
tepid salt water, aided by the syringe if there
be a tight prepuce. The best local application is the warm water-dressing, covering in
the entire genitals; if much swelling and pain

are present, it may be advantageously medicated with lead and opium. As the inflammation subsides, the sore may be dressed with some gently stimulating lotion, as two grains of tannin, the eighth of a grain of sulphate of copper, and half a drachm of laudanum to the ounce of water, a weak mixture of sherry and water, or a solution of nitrate of silver, zinc, or iodide of iron. If the ulcer is disposed to spread, or presents a sloughy or unhealthy aspect, it will be proper to touch it lightly twice a day with the solid nitrate of silver, or a solution of one part of acid nitrate of mercury to four parts of water.

The *constitutional* treatment is rigidly antiphlogistic, or tonic and supporting, according to the particular nature of the case. The bowels should receive early attention; the skin be kept moist; and pain be allayed by anodynes. Perfect recumbency should be observed until the parts are nearly healed. If mercury be required, the best forms will be calomel and blue mass, in small doses twice a day, with a vigilant eye to their effects, ptyalism being studiously avoided in every case.

If *bubo* supervene, the treatment must be

prompt and efficient, with a view to the prevention of further mischief. Recumbency, the topical use of iodine with warm water-dressing medicated with lead and opium, light diet, and the antimonial and saline mixture constitute the most appropriate measures. If matter form, an early and free incision is made, and the part afterward treated as a common sore, the granulating process being promoted by mild means. Mercury is carefully withheld, at all events in the early stage of the disease.

The army is no place for soldiers laboring under secondary or tertiary syphilis; the sooner they are dismissed from the service the better, especially if they are volunteers.

Ophthalmia is one of the annoyances of the soldier's life. Liable to be caused by cold, it is capable of assuming several varieties of form, and sometimes prevails extensively as an epidemic. The granular and purulent, in particular, are to be feared, as they frequently destroy the sight, and even the eye, in a few days, occasioning intense suffering. To ascertain the condition of the parts, the lids must always be gently

12*

everted with a probe or the finger. The greatest cleanliness should be observed in these affections; the patients should, if possible, be sequestered, at all events not be permitted to use the same basins and towels; the light should be excluded from the apartment; and the general and local treatment should either be strictly antiphlogistic or of a mixed character, partly antiphlogistic and partly stimulant. The applications should be of the mildest description, especially those intended for the inflamed surface. The syringe is frequently used to wash away the secretions. Strong collyria generally do immense harm in all forms and stages of ophthalmia. Blood may be taken from the arm, or by cups or leeches from the temples, if the symptoms are unusually urgent and the patient plethoric. In rheumatic inflammation of the eye, colchicum and morphia, given freely at bedtime, will be of immense service.

When *foreign matter* gets into the eye, or becomes imbedded in the cornea, speedy removal must be effected, and the parts afterward treated with rest, cold or tepid bathing, gentle aperients, and seclusion from light.

Particles of steel and other sharp bodies are picked out with the point of a delicate bistoury, or cataract needle. The effects of lime and other alkalies are neutralized by syringing the eye freely with a weak solution of vinegar; those of nitrate of silver, with a weak solution of common salt, a thorough coating of olive oil being afterward applied.

Carbuncles, boils, and abscesses, which are of frequent occurrence in army practice, demand prompt attention, both on account of the suffering they induce and the disqualification they may entail for temporary duty. They should be opened early and freely, and no time be lost in amending the general health by gentle mercurial and other purgatives, alterants and tonics, particularly quinine and iron. The most appropriate topical remedies are tincture of iodine and warm water-dressings.

In carbuncles the affected structures, after free division, will generally require the thorough application of some escharotic or detergent stimulant, as Vienna paste, nitric acid, nitrate of silver, or acid nitrate of mercury.

Frost-bite is extremely common among soldiers during the cold, wet weather of winter.

Thousands of the French troops perished from this cause in Russia, during Napoleon's retreat from Moscow. Frost-bite was very prevalent among the English during their first winter in the Crimea, and the French suffered in still greater numbers, as well as more severely. The habit which the men had of sleeping in their wet boots, at one time almost universal, contributed greatly to its production, wet and cold combined diminishing the circulation and vitality of the feet and toes. On the 21st of January, 1855, when the thermometer stood at 5°, not less than 2500 cases of frost-bite were admitted into the French ambulance, and of these 800 died, death in many having no doubt been expedited by the effects of erysipelas, pyemia, and hospital gangrene. Weak and intemperate persons are most apt to have frost-bite and to perish from its effects.

In the treatment, in incipient cases, cloths, wrung out of cold water impregnated with a little spirits of camphor or alcohol, should be applied, or the parts be covered for a few minutes with snow, or immersed in cold water. On no account must they be exposed to warmth, either moist or dry. Excessive reaction is controlled by lead and laudanum lotions, or dilute tincture of iodine. If gangrene occurs, the ordinary measures, local and general, are indicated. All rude manipulation in dressing the injured part greatly aggravates the disease. In general, spontaneous amputation is waited for, experience having shown that operative interference, even when the part is perfectly black, and attached only by a few living shreds, is extremely prone to be productive of excessive pain and constitutional irritation, often proceeding to an alarming extent.

Among the great evils, both of civil and military practice, are *bed-sores*, which, unless the greatest possible precaution be used, are sure to arise during the progress of acute diseases and of severe accidents, necessitating protracted recumbency. The hips and sacral region are their most common sites, with the heel in cases of fractures of the leg. The earlier symptoms are a sense of prickling, as if the part were rubbed with coarse salt, or a burning, itching or smarting pain, with a brownish or livid discoloration of the skin, and slight swelling. Then gangrene ensues, followed by horrible suffering.

To prevent these sores, which often prove destructive to life, when there is already much exhaustion from previous suffering, the posterior surface of the body should be frequently examined, particularly if the patient is in a state of mental torpor, and pains taken to ward off pressure by the use of air cushions and other means. The parts should be sponged several times a day with some alcoholic lotion containing alum, or painted with a weak solution of iodine. If gangrene or ulceration occurs, a yeast or port wine poultice is used, the separation of the slough is aided with the knife, while the granulating process is promoted by the usual remedies.

Ulcers of the leg are causes of disqualification in enlisting, but they sometimes occur after the soldier has entered the service, from fatigue, injury, or undue constriction of the limb. However induced, they should be managed as any other forms of inflammation, recumbency with elevation of the affected parts, tepid water-dressings, a restricted diet, and cooling purgatives constituting the most important elements of the treatment. When the healing process has fairly commenced, the leg should be supported with the roller, or adhesive strips.

As preventive of ulcers of the legs, the limbs should be daily washed in cold water with Castile soap, and no soldier should be permitted to wear garters.

CHAPTER X.

Military Hygiene.

MUCH disease and suffering may be prevented, and many lives saved, by a careful observance of hygienic regulations. There is no question whatever that immense numbers of soldiers everywhere fall victims to their recklessness and the indulgence of their appetites and passions. We would not advocate too much restraint; men are but men everywhere, and soldiers form no exception to the general law. They, like civilians, must have their amusements and recreations. The bow cannot last long, if kept too constantly and too tightly on the stretch. Occasional relaxation is indispensable to health.

Indolence, however, should never be countenanced in any army. Its demoralizing effects, and its influence upon the health of the soldier, have been noticed and commented upon in all ages. "The efficacy," says an eminent military surgeon, in speaking on the subject, "of due attention to the occupation of the mind must never be lost sight of. Many illustrations of its powerful influence, whether for good or evil, whether in resisting or accelerating the inroads of disease, may be found both in ancient and in modern times, from the retreat of the ten thousand Greeks under Xenophon down to the present day. It may be observed that disease goes hand in hand with indolence and inactivity, whether of body or of mind; and that, on the contrary, where the minds of soldiers are agreeably occupied, and their bodies energetically employed, as in the attainment or pursuit of victory, disease is kept in abeyance." It was the observation of another experienced authority in military medical affairs, Mr. Alcock, that "the period of the smallest loss to an army is a victorious and vigorously prosecuted campaign, with frequent battles and much marching;" an assertion corroborative of the facts, long since so painfully realized, that sickness, however induced, destroys incomparably more soldiers than the sword and the musket.

No intemperance, either in eating or drinking, should be tolerated in an army; both are demoralizing, and both predispose to, if not actually provoke, disease. Alcoholic liquors should not be permitted to be used except as medicine, and then only under the immediate direction of the medical officer. The ordinary drink and food should be selected with special reference to their healthful properties. The use of bad water, even for a short time, is invariably productive of mischief. The tea and coffee should be of good quality, and well prepared, to preserve their agreeable flavor and their soothing and refreshing effects. Lager beer, ale, and porter, if sound, are both nourishing and wholesome, if consumed .within judicious limits.

The practice of allowing soldiers spirituous liquors as a portion of their daily rations has, I believe, been pretty generally, if not entirely, abandoned in the European service. Its injurious effects upon the health and morals

of troops have long been deprecated. In the
British army in India, the use of alcoholic
liquors was, at one time, universal, on the
supposition that it had a tendency to counteract the depressing influences of a tropical
climate; the men took their spirits regularly
before breakfast, and not unfrequently several
times during the day, especially if on active
duty; but it was soon found that it produced
quite a contrary impression, causing instead
of preventing debility, and affording a tempt-
ation to general drunkenness, which was followed by insubordination and crime. The
result was that the government abolished the
alcoholic ration system altogether, substituting
coffee and tea, which are now regularly served
once, and often twice a day.

The condition of the 13th Regiment of
Light Infantry, stationed at Jellalabad, during the late insurrection in India, affords a
happy illustration of the salutary effects of
abstinence from spirituous liquors. While the
siege was progressing, the men, during a
period of five months, were entirely debarred
from drinking, and yet their health and courage were most excellent. As soon, however,

as the garrison was relieved, and they began
to indulge in spirits, many of them in a short
time became sick and riotous. The experience of Major-General Wylie, of the Bombay
army, was precisely similar. When the soldiers under his command were quartered in
districts where no liquor could be obtained,
their health, discipline, and morals were all
that could be desired; whereas, under opposite
circumstances, insubordination and disease
prevailed to a frightful extent.

During the Crimean war, coffee and tea
were found to be eminently wholesome and
invigorating, enabling the troops to sustain
fatigue and to resist disease. When the men
were in the trenches, and could not obtain
their usual supplies of these articles, they
became languid, and suffered from dysentery
and diarrhœa. To produce their peculiar sus-
taining and exhilarating effects, coffee and tea
should be taken hot and moderately strong,
with sugar, if not also with cream.

Fresh meats are always preferable to salt,
though good ham and smoked beef may be
taken once a day with advantage as an agreeable change. Fresh fish are always accept-

able. Pickled pork and beef are far from being good articles as a portion of the daily rations. The frequent use of fresh vegetables is indispensable to the health of the soldiery. Ripe fruits are nearly equally so. Without a proper admixture of this kind, dyspepsia, bowel complaints, and scurvy will, sooner or later, inevitably ensue; and woe to the man that is assailed by them! The acids and other properties contained in these substances are indispensable to the healthy condition of the blood and the solids, and the importance of such a diet cannot be too deeply or too frequently impressed upon the attention of every commissariat. Potatoes, rice, hominy, beans, peas, beets, spinach, lettuce, asparagus, radishes, horse-radish, water-cresses, dried peaches and apples, and the different kinds of fruits as they come into season, should be constantly on hand. Soups, both animal and vegetable, are generally grateful to the palate, as well as useful to the system, and should be used whenever the occasion is favorable for their preparation.

Eggs, butter, milk, and butter-milk should be freely indulged in whenever they can be

procured. Serious disease is often engen-
dered by bad bread and biscuit, and it should
therefore be made a part of the duty of every
medical officer to see that no articles of this
kind are brought into camp.

When in the camp or barracks, the soldier
should take his meals with the same regularity as the ordinary citizen at his home. Neglect of this precaution must necessarily lead
to great bodily inconvenience, and, if long
persisted in, may ultimately lead to serious
disease, especially dyspepsia and other disorders of the digestive apparatus. He should
not disregard regularity even with respect to
his alvine evacuations; for there are few
things more conducive to the preservation of
the health.

The soldier's *dress* should be in strict conformity with the season of the year and the
vicissitudes of the weather. He should, at
no time, be either too hot or too cold, but
always comfortable, changing his apparel with
the alterations of the temperature. Flannel
should be worn next the surface both winter
and summer. The shoes must be thick and
warm, with broad soles; and woolen stockings

will be more comfortable, especially when the troops are marching, than cotton. A thin woolen cap-cover, found so useful in India, will protect the neck from the hot sun, and an oil-silk cap-cover, from the rain. In very wet weather the shoulders might be defended with a cape of oil-cloth.

Frequent *ablutions* will largely contribute to the comfort of the soldier and the preservation of his health. They should be performed at least once a day, the best time being late in the afternoon or in the evening just before retiring. The feet, in particular, should be often washed, especially in marching, for reasons which need not be dwelt upon here. The under-shirt should be changed every night, and frequently washed, to promote the healthy state of the skin.

Exposure to the hot sun, to cold and wet, must alike be avoided. Sojourning in malarious regions will be certain to be punished by an attack of neuralgia or intermittent fever.

All *offals* should be promptly removed from the camp, and carried to a distance of several miles, or be well buried.

The privies should be in the most favorable location as it respects ventilation, and be closed at least every three or four days; or, what is worthy of consideration, every man should be compelled to bury his alvine excretions, as was the custom, in time of war, among the ancient Hebrews, each man being obliged to carry a paddle for that purpose. The emanations from these sources cannot receive too much attention, especially when large masses of men are crowded together, as they are then extremely prone to induce disease.

Finally, the medical officer should make it his special duty to see that every recruit is *vaccinated*, or, if the operation was performed prior to his enlistment, at a distant period, matter should again be inserted, experience having shown that the effects of the virus are, in time, in many instances, totally eradicated from the system. In most of the European armies revaccination is extensively practiced; and it is asserted by Stromeyer that during the Schleswig-Holstein war, on an average, 38 operations out of 1000 were successful.

It is impossible to bestow too much care and attention upon the selection of the camp ground and the arrangement of the tents, as

a vast deal of the comfort and health of the
soldiers must necessarily depend upon them.
The following judicious remarks upon this
subject are from the pen of an eminent military surgeon, the late Dr. Ballingall, who
served in various campaigns, and who was for
many years, as stated elsewhere, Professor of
Military Surgery in the University of Edin-
burgh.

"A camp," says Ballingall, "is most advantageously situated on a gentle declivity,
on a dry soil, and in the vicinity of a run-
ning stream. In order to ascertain the state
of the ground it may sometimes be necessary
to dig into it to some extent; for, although
apparently dry on the surface, it may be
found sufficiently wet at the depth of a few
feet; and if so, ought, if possible, to be
changed, particularly if an encampment is
to be stationary. A camp should never be
formed on ground recently occupied, nor on
a field of battle where much carnage has recently occurred. Many favorable spots are
to be found on the banks of rivers, which,
perhaps, upon the whole, afford the most
eligible sites. We must yet bear in mind

that, when the banks of the rivers are low,
or the country subject to periodical rains or
sudden inundations from the melting of snow
on contiguous mountains, there may be a very
serious danger from this cause. Against the
danger of such a position, we are cautioned
in Mezerey's 'Médecine d'Armée,' which
states a case in which the Austrian army
lost 500 men and 200 horse from a sudden
inundation of this kind."

When damp ground or a low situation is
unavoidable, it should be abandoned as soon
as possible for a better, and, in the mean time,
the greatest care should be taken to protect
the soldiers from damp and wet with straw or
other suitable means.

An army has been known to suffer severely
from disease contracted in a malarious region.
Against such a calamity useful information
may often be elicited from the people of the
neighborhood, especially physicians conver-
sant with insalubrious sites.

When an army is obliged to remain for a
long time stationary, an occasional change of
camp will be greatly conducive to health,
although such change should involve a good

deal of labor and temporary inconvenience. A camp under such circumstances should, at all events, be frequently ventilated, and kept constantly clean, a pure atmosphere being of paramount importance to health and comfort. It may often be difficult to do this, but it must, nevertheless, be done; the welfare of the service absolutely demands it, and no medical officer honestly performs his duty unless he interests himself personally in these matters. "The most obvious and perfect way," says Ballingall, "of thoroughly airing the tents is by shifting them occasionally, and exposing the straw, blankets, and soldier's clothing to the open air; the necessity of frequently changing the straw, and enforcing cleanliness in camp in every possible way, are circumstances too obvious to require any effort of reasoning to enforce. With this view the slaughtering of cattle, and everything likely to create noxious or putrid effluvia, ought to be conducted without the camp, and on the side of it opposite to that from which the wind generally blows."

The demoralizing influence of a camp life is well known, and I am convinced that there

is nothing so well calculated to counteract
this influence as rigid discipline, reasonable
activity of mind and body, strict temperance,
both in eating and drinking, and frequent
religious worship. Every regiment should
have its chaplains, not less than its medical
officers, not only with a view of restraining
vice and promoting morality, but of affording
to the poor soldier, away from home and
friends, in the hour of his mortal extremity,
those consolations which the minister of the
gospel alone knows how to impart. The
mitigation of the horrors and miseries of
war, not less than the tendencies of the age
in which we live, absolutely demand such a
provision.

CHAPTER XI.

Disqualifying Diseases.

TROOPS, whether regulars or volunteers,
should include no men that are not perfectly
qualified, both physically and mentally, for
the hardships of the public service. They

should, in a word, be perfectly sound, or, what is the same thing, free from all defects, congenital or acquired. It is for this reason that they are always subjected to a most thorough examination by the recruiting or regimental surgeon. This examination is, as a general rule, a great deal more rigid in the regular than in the volunteer service. In the former, the regulations are such that, if the recruit is not found to be sound after he has been inspected by the regular army surgeon, the expense incident to his enlistment and transportation falls upon the medical officer who committed the oversight.

An examination of the kind here mentioned demands both time, patience, and skill. In order to make it thorough, the candidate must be completely stripped, so that if any disease or defect in the exterior of the body exist it may be at once rendered apparent. The examination, however, must not be limited to the exterior; it must embrace also the interior. The disqualifying affections may be arranged according to the organs and regions in which they are seated, under separate heads :—

1. The eye and ear. 2. The brain, as the seat of intellect. 3. The lungs and heart. 4. The stomach, bowels, anus, liver, and spleen. 5. The kidneys, bladder, and urethra. 6. The testicles. 7. The exterior of the abdomen. 8. The limbs, including the joints.

The diseases which unfit a man for military service are defects of sight, of hearing, and of speech; weakness of intellect; paralysis; epilepsy; hernia; hydrocele; varicocele; imperfect development or absence of the testes; hemorrhoids, anal fistule, and fissure of the anus; unusual protuberance of the abdomen; organic lesion of the internal organs; large tumors; aneurism; varix of the extremities; ulcers, or large scars indicative of their former existence; bad corns; bunions; overlapping toes; flatfootedness; deformity of the hands and fingers; contractions from burns or other causes; badly united fractures; unreduced dislocations; diseased joints; loss of the incisor and canine teeth; serious disfigurement of the features; spinal curvature; ill-formed shoulders; habits

14

of intemperance; diminutive stature or excessive overgrowth.

In the regular army no man is enlisted under the age of eighteen or over that of forty-five. In the volunteer service, similar regulations obtain, although they are not so rigidly enforced.

Recruiting surgeons, after having examined a candidate for enlistment, are obliged to certify, on honor, that they consider him, in their opinion, to be free from all bodily defects, and mental infirmity, which would, in any way, disqualify him for performing the duties of a soldier.

When men become disqualified for service, in consequence of disease or accident, a surgeon's certificate is also required, in order to aid them afterward in procuring a pension and exemption from ordinary military duties. The affections which may justify a soldier in applying for a release from further service are organic visceral lesions, deafness, blindness, mental imbecility, lameness, large herniæ, and such mutilations as interfere with the proper handling of the sword and musket.

CHAPTER XII.

Feigned Diseases.

SOLDIERS, influenced by a desire to quit the service, to revisit their homes, or evade active duty, will not hesitate, at times, to play the part of impostors, feigning diseases, or even inflicting upon themselves more or less serious injuries, with the hope of accomplishing their designs. This deception, technically called malingering, would be of comparatively little consequence if it were always, or even generally, confined to a few members of a regiment; but when it is remembered that it is liable to become epidemic, spreading from individual to individual, it assumes a deep importance, well calculated to arouse the attention both of the medical officer and of the military commander. Its effects, then, become eminently demoralizing to the service, which, if proper care be not employed to detect and punish it, might seriously suffer, especially when such an outbreak occurs on

the eve of a battle. Great ingenuity is often
displayed by malingerers, requiring no little
vigilance and skill on the part of the surgeon
for its successful exposure, and yet it is not
less necessary for his own credit than for the
honor of the service that he should not permit himself to be deceived.

The number of diseases, imitated by this
class of dissemblers, is surprisingly great, and
there is also quite a list of self-inflicted injuries. Among the former are various mental
diseases, as mania and imbecility; deafness;
amaurosis; epilepsy; paralysis; hæmatemesis; hæmoptysis; gastritis; dysentery and
diarrhœa; affections of the heart; rheumatism; lumbago; wry-neck; contractions of
the joints; incontinence of urine; bloody
urine; and stone in the bladder: among the
latter ophthalmia, opacity of the cornea,
œdema of the limbs, wounds, and amputations of the fingers.

Space will not permit me to enter into any
details respecting this important subject. I
shall, therefore, content myself with a pre-
sentation of such facts as may be supposed to
be of special practical interest.

First of all, the medical officer should weigh
well in his own mind the nature of the disease
for which a soldier applies for a certificate of
discharge, or inability to perform duty. If
the case is one of recent standing, it will be
well not to come to too hasty a conclusion as
to its diagnosis; it should be examined and
re-examined before any definite opinion is
given. Day by day new facts may be developed, revealing the true character of the affection. If the patient is really sick, or affected
with some serious chronic disorder, his general
appearance will hardly fail to afford some evi-
dence of its existence. The pallor of the
countenance, the functional disturbance of
the suffering organ, the bodily prostration,
the want of appetite, and the gradual emaciation will almost unerringly point to the nature
and seat of the disease. When, on the other
hand, the malady is simulated, all, or nearly
all, the usual phenomena of disease will be
absent. Imposters, moreover, are generally
very zealous in talking about their disorders,
or in obtruding them upon the notice of
their surgeons, whereas those who are really
sick and suffering make comparatively little

complaint. A malingerer may often be detected by carefully watching his movements, coming suddenly upon him when he is asleep or when his attention is directed to some one else, tickling his foot when he feigns paralysis, or pricking his back when he pretends to be laboring under lumbago. Sometimes a determined threat will promptly restore him to a sense of his duty, as the application of the actual cautery in incontinence of urine, rheumatism of the joints, or mental imbecility. Now and then the exhibition, in rapidly repeated doses, of a nauseous draught, answers the purpose. Whatever expedients be employed, the surgeon cannot exercise too much address, otherwise he will be almost sure to be baffled.

Mental alienation, or *mania,* unless the result of inebriation and of acute disease, generally comes on gradually, being preceded by a marked change in the moral character of the individual, loss of appetite and sleep, and other evidences of general disorder.

Genuine *deafness* is also gradual in its approaches, and, when fully established, is invariably attended by a peculiar listless state

of the countenance with more or less change
of the voice. Before a final decision is given,
a careful inspection of the ears should be
made, to ascertain whether there is any obstruction or appearance of matter. The unexpected discharge of a pistol, in a case of
feigned deafness, might suddenly decide the
diagnosis.

Amaurosis may be simulated by the internal use of belladonna, or by the direct application of this article to the eye, causing
dilatation and immobility of the pupil. These
effects are often accompanied by unnatural
vascularity of the conjunctiva, and they generally disappear spontaneously in a few days.
In genuine amaurosis, too, there is always a
dilated condition of the vessels of the eye.

Feigned *epilepsy* differs from the real in
the absence of lividity of the countenance,
the want of froth at the mouth, and the
partial character of the convulsions. The
pupil does not contract as in the genuine
disease, the general sensibility is unimpaired,
the tongue is not injured, the nails are not
discolored, the hand, if opened, is again firmly
shut, and the individual often watches with

his eye the impression the attack is making
upon the by-standers. The application of a
heated case-knife, or of a cloth wrung out of
hot water, often speedily reveals the imposition.

Paralysis is frequently imitated, but is
generally easily detected, simply by watching
the patient, tickling his feet when he is asleep,
or threatening him with the hot iron. The
disease, when it attacks the lower extremity,
is nearly always caused by apoplexy, and is
then generally associated with mental weakness and difficulty of articulation. Partial
paralysis of the upper extremity is frequently
induced by lying upon the arm, by suppres-
sion of the cutaneous perspiration, and disease
of the spinal cord.

Hæmatemesis may be simulated by swallowing blood, or an infusion of logwood, and
ejecting the fluid afterward by vomiting. It
should be recollected that the real disease is
almost invariably connected with serious organic lesion, as ulceration of the stomach,
induration and enlargement of the liver, or
visceral obstruction, and that the patient,
consequently, will exhibit all the characteristics of a sick person.

Soldiers sometimes counterfeit *hæmoptysis* by cutting the gums, or chewing substances impregnated with coloring matter. A case is related by Guthrie, in which a man, for this purpose, swallowed a piece of cork full of pins. The immediate effect was hæmoptysis, and the remote one death by wounding the carotid artery.

Gastritis may be simulated by spontaneous vomiting, a faculty possessed by some persons, and by pretended pain in the epigastric region. The attack in general speedily yields to a large sinapism and a brisk emetic.

Dysentery and *diarrhœa* are occasionally feigned by exciting, artificially, irritation of the rectum, by mixing blood with the alvine evacuations, or by borrowing the discharges of persons actually affected with these diseases. In genuine dysentery and diarrhœa there are always well-marked constitutional phenomena, which are of course absent in the spurious. Careful watching of the patient and compelling him to use a close stool will soon remove any doubt that may exist respecting the nature of the case.

Disease of the *heart*, in the form of palpi-

tation, may, it is said, be produced by the use
of hellebore.   Mr. Hutchinson, of England,
refers to an epidemic of this kind among the
members of the Marine Artillery.   Organic
cardiac disease could easily be detected with
the stethoscope.

Rheumatism being a very common disease
among soldiers, is often counterfeited; but
the cheat is of easy detection when it is recollected that the real affection, especially
the acute form, is attended with more or less
swelling and constitutional disturbance.

When *lumbago* is made the subject of deception, the attack seldom long withstands
the application of rash remedies, or the
threatened use, if speedy relief do not arise,
of the hot iron.

Contraction of the *joints*, a not unfrequent
source of imposition, is easily detected by the
use of anæsthetics, or simply by pricking the
parts suddenly with a needle when the patient is off his guard.

When *wry-neck* is simulated, both the
sterno-cleido-mastoid muscles are rendered
rigid by the effort at deception; whereas in

the real disease the contraction is confined to one side.

Incontinence of urine, bloody urine, and stone in the bladder have all been simulated by designing soldiers. The former is said to be at times epidemic, and then its detection is of course easy, as the ordinary disease never assumes such a character. Harsh remedies are the best means of relief. Ballingall states that fictitious cases of incontinence have been successfully treated by the cold bath, by prescribing a few lashes on the loins with the avowed object of strengthening the parts. In the Austrian army the impostor is obliged to do duty with a urinal.

Bloody urine has been provoked by injecting blood into the bladder, and by scarifying the urethra.

Calculus is almost unknown among soldiers; it is sometimes attempted to be counterfeited by scraping the walls and throwing the lime into the urinal. When stone actually exists, the sound will generally promptly detect it.

Self-inflicted *injuries* of various kinds are resorted to for the purposes of deception.

Thus malingerers often provoke inflammation
of the eye and temporary opacity of the cornea by means of corrosive sublimate, lime,
tobacco, nitrate of silver, and other irritants.
A great number of men have been known to
suffer from this cause at the same time, as if
the disease were an epidemic.   Ulcers of the
legs are produced by pricking the skin with
pins or needles, frictions with sand, or caustic
applications.   Œdema of the limbs may be
excited by tight ligatures; disease of the
scrotum and testicle, by inflation of the parts
with air.   All such tricks are usually readily
detected by the medical officer and his assistants.

Self-mutilation sometimes amounts to the
destruction of an eye, an entire finger, or
even the greater portion of the hand.   Occasionally it is limited to slight wounds, and the
imposition may then be practiced on an extensive scale, as was the case in the French
army at the battles of Lutzen and Bautzen,
in which nearly 3000 soldiers were slightly
injured in the hands, causing the belief that
the wounds had been voluntarily inflicted.

CHAPTER XIII.

Medical, Surgical, and Dietetic Formulæ.

UNDER this head I propose to notice such formulæ, or medical, surgical, and dietetic preparations, as have been found serviceable in my own practice or in the practice of others.

1.—*General Remedies.*

Among the more simple *purgatives* may be mentioned the following: all drastic articles should, if possible, be excluded from the prescriptions of the military surgeon :—

℞.—Massæ ex Hydrargy. gr. x;
   Pulv. Ipecac. gr. i.
   M. ft. pil. ii.

A mild laxative in dyspepsia and disorders of the stomach and liver.

℞.—Extr. Colocynth. c;
   Massæ ex Hydrargy.
   Pulv. Rhei. v. Jalapæ, āā gr. x;
   Ant. et Potassæ Tart. gr. $\frac{1}{16}$.
   M. ft. pil. v.

15

An active, antibilious purgative, from three to five being an ordinary dose. Calomel may be substituted for the blue mass, if there is much disorder of the liver and secretions.

The safest *emetics* are ipecacuanha, infusion of eupatorium, perfoliatum, and mustard and common salt, an even tablespoonful of each to half a pint of tepid water, one-half to be taken at once, the remainder, if necessary, in fifteen minutes. Sulphate of copper or zinc will afford the most prompt emetic effect in case of great urgency, as in poisoning.

The following formula will be found very serviceable in the earlier stages of most inflammatory affections, especially the cutaneous, articular, and traumatic, unaccompanied by disease of the alimentary canal :—

R/.—Ant. et Potass. Tart. gr. iss ;
  Magnesiæ Sulph. ʒi ;
  Morphiæ Sulph. gr. ss ;
  Sacch. Albi. ʒii ;
  Aquæ Destil. ʒvi. M.

This is the antimonial and saline mixture of which repeated mention occurs in the preceding pages, and which I am in the daily habit of prescribing in my surgical as well as medical practice. It may be rendered depressant by the addition to each dose—which is half an ounce, repeated every two or three hours—of from three to eight drops of the tincture of veratrum viride; anodyne, or diaphoretic, by laudanum, or morphia; antiperiodic, by quinine; anti-gonorrhœal, by copaiba, gum-arabic being used, in the latter case, as one of the ingredients; and anti-rheumatic, by colchicum. If quinine be used, the addition of aromatic sulphuric acid will be required, which is also an excellent solvent of the salts.

℞.—Vini Colchici Sem. ʒi;
  Morphiæ Sulph. gr. ss;
  Potassæ Carbon. gr. x;
  Aquæ Destil. ʒss. M.

In rheumatic and gouty affections, taken at bedtime, and followed by a mild aperient next morning.

The following will be found to be pleasant and efficient *diaphoretics*:—

℞.—Spirit. Mindereri, ʒiv;
  Sp. Æther. Nitrici. ʒii;
  Morphiæ Acet. gr. i. M. S.

Tablespoonful every two or three hours. If there be much heat of surface, we may add

to each dose the eighth, twelfth, or fifteenth
of a grain of tartar emetic.

    ℞.—Potassæ Carbon. ℥i;
        Morphiæ Sulph. gr. i;
        Sacch. Albi. ℥ii;
        Suc. Limonis recent. ℥ii;
        Aquæ Menth. v. Destil. ℥iiiss;
        Sp. Æther. Nitrici. ℥ss.   M. S.
Tablespoonful every hour or two.

The effervescing draught, so valuable in
irritability of the stomach, is composed as
follows :—

    ℞.—Suc. Limonis recent. ℥ji;
        Sacch. Albi. ℥jiss;
        Aquæ Destil. ℥ji.   M.

    ℞.—Potassæ Carbon. ℥i;
        Aquæ Destil. ℥ji.   M.
Put two tablespoonsful of the lemonade with
one of the alkaline solution, and let the mixture be drunk while effervescing, repeating
the dose at pleasure.

As *antiperiodics* quinine and arsenic are
the main reliance of the modern practitioner.
The former may be given by itself, in pill or
solution, in doses varying from two to ten
grains, according to the urgency of the case

or the state of the system. My usual dose is ten grains every eight, ten, or twelve hours, until the paroxysm is arrested. If the symptoms are unusually violent, we need not hesitate to administer fifteen or even twenty grains at a dose, being of course careful to watch the effects, which will generally be more pleasant if a little morphia be combined with the quinine.

In chronic, or frequently-recurring intermittent and neuralgic affections, arsenic forms a valuable, and; indeed, in many cases, an indispensable addition; also iron, if there be evidences of anæmia. I prefer myself the arsenious acid to Fowler's solution, convinced that it is much more efficacious and at the same time less apt to cause nausea and anasarca. The following formula will be found advantageous :—

    ℞.—Acid. Arseniosi, gr. iss;

        Quiniæ Sulph.

        Ferri Sulph. āā ʒi;

        Morphiæ Sulph. gr. i;

        Extr. Nucis Vomicæ, ℈i.

    M. ft. pil. xxx.

S. One every five, six, or eight hours.

Quinine is also one of the best *tonics,* and it may always be beneficially combined with other articles, as iron, gentian, quassia, nux vomica, and capsicum. The fluid extracts and aromatic tinctures of bark and gentian will also be found useful. One of the best chalybeate preparations is the tincture of the chloride of iron, in doses of from twenty to twenty-five drops three or four times daily.

Expectorants constitute a large class of remedial agents, but they nearly all derive their active principles from the admixture of tartar emetic, ipecacuanha, or squills. They may generally be usefully combined with potassa and anodynes, being rendered palatable by syrup or sugar.

Nurses should be familiar with the manner of administering *enemata* or injections, as frequent occasions arise for their employment. They may be cathartic, as when they are designed to empty the lower bowel, or to promote the action of other remedies; stimulant, as in case of excessive exhaustion; nutritive, as when food cannot be taken by the mouth; anodyne, when it is wished to allay pain and induce sleep.

A *cathartic* effect may readily be induced by an injection of a pint and a half of cold water, or water in which a little ground mustard or common salt has been stirred, a mixture of warm water and castor oil; or an infusion of senna, or senna and Epsom salts. Turpentine is particularly indicated when the bowels are distended with flatus.

Stimulating injections may be made of brandy, alcohol, mustard, salt, or spirits of camphor or turpentine, mixed with more or less water; and they are often extremely serviceable in promoting reaction.

Nutritive enemata may be necessary in the low stages of fever, and in gunshot and other injuries attended with lesion of the gullet. The best ingredients are essence of beef, strong beef-tea, brandy, or brandy and milk, introduced in small quantity so as not to oppress and irritate the rectum.

Anodyne injections may consist of laudanum, black drop, morphia, hyoscyamus, or belladonna, either alone, or variously combined, and administered with about two ounces of tepid water, or some demulcent fluid.

The best *syringe* now in use is the gutta-percha, which is not liable to be deranged, and which has the additional advantage of durability. It should be of various capacities, from eight to sixteen ounces, according to the intention to be fulfilled by it. The nozzle must be well oiled previously to its introduction, and care taken that no air be pushed into the bowel.

2.—*Topical Remedies.*

℞.—Tinct. Iodinæ,
          Sp. Vini Rectific. āā ʒj.   M.
To be applied with a large camel-hair pencil, or cloth mop.   I hardly ever use the pure tincture of iodine for local purposes.

℞.—Plumbi Subacet. ʒj ;
          Pulv. Opii, ʒj.   M.
To be put in half a gallon of *hot* water, and the solution to be used warm or cold, as may be deemed best.   Laudanum may be substituted for the opium.

℞.—Pulv. Ammoniæ Hydrochlor. ʒj ;
     "   Potassæ Nitrat. ʒij ;
     "   Opii, ʒj.   M.
To be used as the preceding, being particu-

larly valuable, in inflammation of the joints, on unbroken surfaces.

The *warm water-dressing* consists of warm water, simple or medicated with laudanum, acetate of lead, or any other ingredient that may be desired, applied upon flannel or muslin cloths, properly folded, and covered with oiled silk, to confine heat and moisture.

The *cold water-dressing* is composed of cold water, also simple or medicated, applied with cloths, the parts being constantly exposed to the air to promote evaporation. The cloths are wet whenever they become heated or dryish, the water being pressed upon them from a sponge.

Water-dressings, if long continued, will occasionally cause irritation, itching, and pustulation of the skin, rendering it necessary to replace them with cataplasms, or other soothing remedies.

Among *poultices* decidedly the best, for ordinary purposes, are the flaxseed and slippery elm. The former is made by mixing a suitable quantity of linseed meal with hot, or, what is still better, boiling water, and rapidly stirring it into a thick mush-like consistence. The mixture is then spread upon a fold of cloth, in a layer a third of an inch thick, when it is covered with bobinet or gauze to prevent it from adhering to the parts. A piece of oiled silk, larger than the poultices, is placed upon its outer surface, to retain heat and moisture.

The elm, and, in fact, all other cataplasms, are prepared and used upon the same principles as the linseed. Like water-dressings, poultices may be simple or medicated, according to the object proposed. They should be changed at least twice, or, in warm weather, even three or four times in the twenty-four hours.

Adhesive plaster is cut, in the direction of its length, into strips of suitable length and breadth, warmed by holding the back against a smooth vessel, as a pitcher or tin case, and applied in such a manner as to bring the middle of each piece over the wound, the edges of which are, meanwhile, carefully supported by an assistant. A suitable space is left between the strips for drainage. If things progress favorably, substitution need not be made under three or four days. If the wound be

large, only a few of the strips are taken off
at a time, lest, all support being lost, the
edges should be forcibly separated.

Before the soiled dressings are removed,
everything intended for the new should be
prepared, or put in its proper place. The
strips of plaster must be removed with great
gentleness.

If the injured parts are covered with hair,
the surface must always be shaved before the
application of the dressings.

Proper material for *sutures* should always
be kept on hand, ready for use. The silver
wire is the best, as it is less irritating than
any other. Silk, however, answers exceedingly well; the thread should be rather thin,
and be well waxed. Saddler's silk is the article used for the ligation of large arteries.

Among the more common and useful *un-
guents* for dressing wounds, burns, abraded
surfaces, or fissures, are the following:—

℞.—Pulv. Opii, Ʒss;

Pulv. Rhei, Ɖi;

Ung. Cetacei, Ʒi.   M.

To these ingredients may advantageously be
added, in many cases of healing sores, or

eruptions requiring a mild stimulus, a drachm
of the ointment of the nitrate of mercury, a
few drops of nitric acid, two drachms of ointment of acetate of lead, a small quantity of
myrrh, or of balsam of Peru, or from six to
eight grains of sulphate of quinine.

℞.—Ung. Cetacei, ʒi ;

Bismuth. Subnitr. ʒij.   M.

Extremely soothing and valuable in super-
ficial excoriations, slight burns, and eczema-
tous affections.   Turner's cerate may be employed for similar purposes, but should always
be considerably diluted.

The best *disinfectants* are the chloride of
soda, chloride of lime, Labarraque's solution,
and the hypermanganate of potassa, of which
an abundant supply should always be on hand
in every hospital, free use of it being made,
by sprinkling and otherwise, upon the dressings, as well as upon the bedding and the
rooms.

The *sponges* about a hospital should be of
the softest kind, perfectly clean, and always
ready for use.   The same articles should
never be employed upon different persons,

especially where there are foul or specific
sores, as contagion might thus be communi-
cated by direct inoculation, as has, for example, so often happened during the prevalence
of hospital gangrene.

3.—Dietetic Preparations.

The diet of the sick-room has slain its
thousands and tens of thousands. Broths,
and slops, and jellies, and custards, and pti-
sans are usually as disgusting as they are per-
nicious. Men worn out by disease and injury
must have nutritious and concentrated food.
The ordinary preparations for the sick are, in
general, not only not nutritious, but insipid
and flatulent. Nitrogenous food is what is
needed, even if the quantity taken be very
small. Animal soups are among the most
efficient supporters of the exhausted system,
and every medical man should know how to
give directions for their preparation. The
life of a man is his food. Solid articles are
of course withheld in acute diseases, in their
earlier stages, but when the patient begins to
convalesce they are frequently borne with

16

impunity, and greatly promote recovery. All animal soups should be made of lean meat; and their nutritious properties, as well as their flavor, may be much increased by the addition of some vegetable substance, as rice or barley. If the stomach is very weak, they may be diluted, or seasoned with pepper.

Essence of beef, so frequently given in the low stages of fever, and in the exhaustion consequent upon severe injuries and operations, is prepared by cutting from a quarter to half a pound of lean beef into thin pieces, and putting it into a wide-mouthed porter bottle, corked tightly, and placed in a kettle of cold water, which is then heated till it boils. After it has been digested in this way for a few hours, the juice is decanted, and seasoned with salt and pepper, wine or brandy.

Beef tea, much less nourishing than beef essence, is made by putting a quarter of a pound of lean beef in a pint and a half of water, and boiling it for fifteen minutes, a few blades of mace being added during the process, and the fluid well skimmed.

To make *chicken broth* requires half a

young chicken and a quart of cold water, with a teaspoonful of rice or barley, the whole being slowly boiled for two hours under cover, with proper skimming.

Chicken jelly is prepared by putting a chicken, cut up and all the bones broken, in a stone jar, closely covered, and retained in boiling water for three hours and a half. The liquor is then strained, and seasoned with salt and mace.

Vegetable soup is composed of two Irish potatoes, one onion, and a piece of bread, with a quart of water, boiled down to a pint in a closely-covered vessel, a little celery or parsley being introduced near the close of the operation. Salt and pepper are added at pleasure.

To form *rice jelly* a quarter of a pound of rice flour and twice that quantity of loaf sugar are boiled in a quart of water until the whole becomes a glutinous mass, when the jelly is strained off and flavored.

Sago jelly is composed of four tablespoonsful of sago, one quart of water, juice and rind of one lemon, and enough sugar to render it

agreeable.   After the mixture has stood half
an hour, it is boiled until all the particles are
entirely dissolved, the mass being constantly
stirred.

Oatmeal gruel is composed of two large
spoonsful of oatmeal and half a pint of milk,
stirred into one pint of boiling water, and
allowed to simmer for thirty minutes, when it
is strained through a hair sieve. *Cornmeal
gruel* is prepared in a similar manner.

Arrow-root pap consists of a large tablespoonful of this substance made into a paste
with a little cold water, which is then stirred
into a pint of boiling water, and kept on the
fire for five minutes.   The nourishing properties of arrow-root pap may be heightened by
using milk instead of water in its preparation.

Milk toast is often much relished by the
sick; and there is a very excellent jelly for
invalids made of a thinly sliced and slightly
toasted penny roll, boiled in a quart of water
until it becomes a glutinous mass, when it
should be strained upon a few shavings of
lemon-peel.

The flavor and efficacy of the various

dietetic preparations here described may be greatly increased by the addition of mace, lemon, wine, or brandy. When salt, or salt and pepper are used, the patient's own taste should be consulted. Great care should be employed in making these compounds that they are not scorched. To prevent this a double boiler should be used.

Milk-punch, an excellent article when a stimulant is required in conjunction with a nutrient, is made by mixing good brandy with cold, fresh milk, in the proportion of about one ounce of the former to half a pint of the latter. Sugar and nutmeg may be added to make the mixture palatable.

Wine-whey, well made, may be rendered of great service to the sick. It is prepared by adding to a pint of fresh milk, as soon as it reaches the boiling point, as much good Madeira or sherry as will coagulate it. The mixture is then strained, and sweetened or flavored for use.

The best *wines* for the sick are Madeira, port, and sherry. In cases of gastric irritation, champagne sometimes produces an ex-

16*

cellent effect, quieting the stomach as well as the system at large.

Egg-nog consists of an egg, the white and yolk of which are beaten up separately; half a pint of cold water with a little loaf-sugar is then added, together with two tablespoonsful of brandy.

APPENDIX.

THE subjoined regulations respecting the admission of Medical Men into the Army of the United States, and the pay of Army Surgeons, were issued by the War Department in March, 1857 :—

No person can receive the appointment of ASSISTANT SURGEON in the ARMY OF THE UNITED STATES, unless he shall have been examined and approved by an ARMY MEDICAL BOARD, to consist of not less than three SURGEONS or ASSISTANT SURGEONS, to be designated for that purpose by the Secretary of War; nor can any person receive the appointment of SURGEON IN THE ARMY OF THE UNITED STATES, unless he shall have served five years as an ASSISTANT SURGEON, and unless, also, he shall have been examined by an ARMY MEDICAL BOARD, constituted as aforesaid.

BOARDS OF MEDICAL EXAMINERS are convened at such times as the wants of the service render it necessary, when selections are made by the Secretary of War of the number of applicants to be ex-

(183)

amined for appointment of ASSISTANT SURGEON. To
the persons thus selected, invitations are given to
present themselves to the BOARD for examination.
These invitations state the time and place of meeting
of the BOARD.

APPLICANTS must be between 21 and 28 years of
age. The BOARD will scrutinize rigidly the moral
habits, professional acquirements, and physical qualifications of the candidates, and report favorably in
no case admitting of a reasonable doubt.

The BOARD will report the respective merits of
the candidates in the several branches of the examination, and their relative merit from the whole;
agreeably whereto, if vacancies happen within two
years thereafter, they will receive appointments and
take rank in the Medical Corps.

AN APPLICANT failing at one examination, may be
allowed a second, after two years; but never a third.

APPLICATIONS must be addressed to the SECRE-
TARY OF WAR; must state the residence of the applicant, and the date and place of his birth. They
must also be accompanied by respectable testimo-
nials of his possessing the moral and physical qualifications requisite for filling creditably the responsible station, and for performing ably the arduous and
active duties of an officer of the Medical Staff.

No ALLOWANCE is made for the expenses of persons undergoing these examinations, as they are indispensable prerequisites to appointment; but those
who are approved and receive appointments will be
entitled to transportation on obeying their first order.

The pay and emoluments of Surgeons and Assistant Surgeons are shown by the following table.

RANK.	Pay per month.	No. of rations per day.	Amount of rations per month.	No. of horses for which forage is allowed.	Amount for forage per month.	SERVANTS.					Aggregate amount receivable.
						No. for which pay is allowed.	Amount allowed for pay per month.	Amount allowed for clothing per month.	Amount allowed for rations per month.	Total amount allowed per month.	
Assistant Surgeon, under five years' service....	$53 33	4	$36	1	$8	1	$12	$2 50	$9	$23 50	$120 83
Assistant Surgeon, over five years' service......	70 00	4	36	1	8	1	12	2 50	9	23 50	137 50
Assistant Surgeon, over ten years' service......	70 00	8	72	1	8	1	12	2 50	9	23 50	173 50
Surgeon, under ten years' service............	80 00	4	36	3	24	2	24	5 00	18	47 00	187 00
Surgeon, over ten years' service..............	80 00	8	72	3	24	2	24	5 00	18	47 00	223 00

The allowance for forage and servants is paid to the Surgeons and Assistant Surgeons only when they actually employ and keep in service the number of servants and horses charged for.

In addition to the above, Surgeons and Assistant Surgeons are allowed an additional ration per day, after the termination of every five years' service.

The Surgeons and Assistant Surgeons of the Volunteer Military service are commissioned by the Governor of the State in which they are enrolled, their appointment being received either directly from him or from the officers of their regiment. It is obvious that the candidates for admission should be subjected to a rigid examination before a competent Medical Board; and there is reason to believe that, in view of the great importance of the subject, such a Board will soon be established in every State. The pay of the Surgeons—of whom there are two in each regiment, a Chief and his Assistant—of the volunteer forces is the same as in the regular army, when mustered into service. The salary of the Surgeon-General is $2740 a year.

STROMEYER AND ESMARCH

ON

GUNSHOT INJURIES.

GUNSHOT FRACTURES. By Dr. Louis Stromeyer.
RESECTION IN GUNSHOT INJURIES. By Dr.
Friedrich Esmarch.

One vol. 12mo. 75 cents.

In the present volume are combined two valuable treatises on Gunshot Injuries, by eminent German surgeons, forming a book that army surgeons in particular will prize highly.—*Buffalo Express.*

Dr. Stromeyer was Surgeon-in-Chief of the Schleswig-Holstein army, in the campaign of 1849, against the Danes. Dr. Esmarch accompanied Dr. Stromeyer in this campaign, which, if not on a very extensive scale, was yet quite extensive enough to enable their intelligent surgeons to frequently exercise their skill and obtain a practical knowledge of the subjects they treat of in this book—one interesting and valuable to all army surgeons.—*New York Post.*

MAXIMS AND INSTRUCTIONS

ON THE

A R T   O F   W A R.

MAXIMS, ADVICE, AND INSTRUCTIONS ON THE Art of War; or, A Practical Military Guide for the use of Soldiers of all Arms and of all Countries. Translated from the French by Captain Lendy, Director of the Practical Military College, late of the French Staff, etc. etc.

One vol. 18mo. 75 cents.

J. B. Lippincott & Co.'s Military Publications.

McCLELLAN'S ARMIES OF EUROPE.

THE ARMIES OF EUROPE; comprising descriptions in detail of the Military Systems of England, France, Russia, Prussia, Austria, and Sardinia. Adapting their advantages to all arms of the United States Service. Embodying the Report of Observations in Europe during the Crimean war, as Military Commissioner from the United States Government in 1855–56. By Geo. B. McClellan, Major-General U.S.A. Originally published under the direction of the War Department, by order of Congress. 1 vol. 8vo. Illustrated with a fine steel Portrait and several hundred engravings. $3.50.

"Of the publications occasioned by the crisis, doubtless the most important is the reissue, in a form adapted to general circulation, of the great report on the armies of Europe of Geo. B. McClellan, now commander-in-chief of the armies of the United States."—*The Methodist.*

"The young captain of calvary is now a major-general, and to his hands the destinies of our nation are in a great measure intrusted; and his book will now be recognized as a popular necessity, and find its way into the hands of the multitude."—*New York Times.*

"The work contains all that vast body of detailed information pertaining to the equipment, direction, and care of our military forces, which is actually indispensable to every officer in the army, and may be of the greatest service to every private in the ranks."—*Boston Transcript.*

"The book is invaluable to military men from the technical information and the sagacious views it presents. It is of the greatest interest to the public in general, from the striking revelation it makes of the character and genius of its modest and gifted author."—*Boston Journal.*

"The volume will be of great importance to the host of young officers who are ambitious to excel in the art or profession to which they have now devoted themselves."—*New York Sun.*

McCLELLAN'S

UNITED STATES CAVALRY.

REGULATIONS AND INSTRUCTIONS FOR THE FIELD SERVICE of the United States Cavalry in Time of War.

BY GEO. B. McCLELLAN,

MAJOR-GENERAL U. S. ARMY.

One vol. 12mo.   Fully Illustrated. $1.50.

To which is added the Basis of Instruction for the U. S. Cavalry, from the Authorized Tactics,—including the formation of regiments and squadrons, the duties and posts of officers, lessons in the training and use of the horse,—illustrated by numerous diagrams, with the signals and calls now in use. Also, instructions for officers and non-commissioned officers on outpost and patrol duty. With a drill for the use of cavalry as skirmishers, mounted and dismounted.

"The volume is a complete manual for this arm of the service, and its value cannot be overrated. Gen. McClellan enjoyed almost unequaled facilities for perfecting himself in a knowledge of the modern European systems of tactics while a member of the Commission sent by our Government to the Old World, and he has concentrated the results of his observations within this volume. No work on the subject could have more weight, and we can think of none which will be more useful while the country is prosecuting the war for its existence."—*Evening Bulletin.*

"The precepts contained in this volume are applicable to every detail of duty which cavalry may be expected to perform in time of war in the field. It could not, therefore, be more valuable or more timely than at present." * * * "Every cavalry soldier should have it in his hands."—*North American.*

"We question whether ever before, in the same compass, so much practical information on the cavalry arm of war was collected. It is a thoroughly complete *vade mecum* for every mounted soldier in the service."—*The Press.*

HARDEE'S TACTICS.

Rifle and Light Infantry Tactics,

For the Exercise and Manœuvres of Troops when acting as Light Infantry or Riflemen.

Prepared under the direction of the War Department,

By Brevet Lieutenant-Colonel W. J. HARDEE, U.S.A.

Two Vols. complete. $1.50.

VOL. I.

Schools of the Soldier and Company; Instruction for Skirmishers.

VOL. II.

School of the Battalion.

This work is a careful revision of the rifle and light infantry tactics for the exercise and manœuvres of troops when acting as light infantry or riflemen. It was prepared, under the direction of the War Department, by Brevet Lieutenant-Colonel WM. J. HARDEE, late Tactical Instructor at West Point. Hardee's Tactics have been adopted as the text-book in the military establishments of nearly every State in the Union, and hold a high rank among military men as of great practical utility in the light infantry arm. The work is prepared in a clear and lucid manner and with numerous pictorial illustrations. The famous Chicago Zouave drill is essentially Hardee's tactics, with the exception of some few fancy movements of no utility except to give a finish to an exhibition drill. The work is printed in clear type, and is invaluable as a book of instruction to our volunteer corps.—*New York Herald*, Jan. 28, 1861.

ORDNANCE MANUAL

---◈---

THE ORDNANCE MANUAL,

For the use of the Officers of the Army and others.

PREPARED UNDER THE DIRECTION OF THE WAR DEPARTMENT.

Third edition. One vol. demi-8vo Fully illustrated
with Engravings on steel. $2.50.

CONTENTS. --Chap. I. Ordnance. II. Shot and Shell.
III. Artillery Carriages. IV. Machines, etc. for Siege
and Garrison Service. V. Artillery Implements and
Equipments. VI. Artillery Harness and Cavalry Equip-
ments. VII. Paints, Lackers, etc. VIII. Small Arms,
Swords, and Accoutrements. IX. Gunpowder, Lightning
Rods. X. Ammunition of all kinds, Fireworks. XI.
Equipment of Batteries for Field, Siege, and Garrison
Service. XII. Mechanical Manœuvres. XIII. Artillery
Practice, Ranges, Penetration, etc. XIV. Materials,
Strength of Materials. XV. Miscellaneous information,
Tables of Weights and Measures, Physical Data, Mathe-
matical Formulæ, Ballistics, Tables, etc.

ORDNANCE DEPARTMENT,
WASHINGTON, Nov. 4, 1861.

HON. S. CAMERON, *Secretary of War.*

It is respectfully recommended that the revised edition of the Ordnance Manual be published for the use of the Army.

WILLIAM MAYNADIER,
Lt. Col. of Ordnance in charge of Bureau

Approved, Nov. 4, 1861.

THOMAS A. SCOTT,
Acting Secretary of War.

This most valuable work to persons engaged in the military service and in the preparation of any of the various military supplies
(the construction of which is given in minute detail,) will also prove
useful to mechanics generally for the valuable tables and miscellaneous information which it contains.

DUFFIELD'S

SCHOOL OF THE BRIGADE.

SCHOOL OF THE BRIGADE, AND EVOLUTIONS
of the Line; or, Rules for the Exercise and Manœuvres of Brigades and Divisions. Designed as a Se-
quel to the United States Infantry Tactics, adopted
May 1, 1861. By WILLIAM W. DUFFIELD, Acting
Brigadier-General Twenty-third Brigade, and Colonel
Ninth Michigan Infantry.

One vol. 18mo. 75 cents.

MAJOR MORDECAI'S REPORT.

REPORT OF THE MILITARY COMMISSION TO EUROPE
IN 1855 AND 1856.
BY MAJOR MORDECAI, OF THE ORDNANCE DEPARTMENT.

To which is appended

Rifled Infantry Arms.

A BRIEF DESCRIPTION OF THE MODERN SYS-
tem of Small Arms, as adopted in the various European Armies. By J. SCHÖN, Captain in the Royal
Saxon Infantry, etc. etc. Second edition, revised and
augmented with Explanatory Plates. Translated from
the German by J. GORGAS, Capt. of Ordnance, U.S.A.

One vol. 4to. Numerous Engravings. $3.50.

SCHALK'S

ART OF WAR.

SUMMARY OF THE ART OF WAR. Written expressly for, and dedicated to, the United States Volunteer Army. By EMIL SCHALK, Officer of Artillery.

One vol. 12mo. Illustrated with beautifully-engraved Maps, Plates, and Diagrams. $1.50.

"Mr. Schalk, in our humble opinion, has admirably succeeded. He has here, in language simple and readily comprehended, unvailed the whole mystery of strategy, tactics, grand tactics, mixed operations, and logistics, including copious historical and professional descriptions of some of the most celebrated battles, marches, and sieges of modern times, with numerous original diagrams and maps of the greatest interest. Mr. Schalk's first grand example of strategy is the war in the United States, presupposing the movements, on both sides, of the campaign now actually in progress. The results at which the writer arrives are so utterly at variance with popular ideas on the subject, and yet so astonishingly in consonance with the actual state of our military chess-board, that the reflecting reader will be startled at their resemblance to a fixed prediction. The positions and forces of the opposing armies, both east and west, are given with singular accuracy, and the very battle-fields which have just become, or are becoming memorable, are marked beforehand. The diagrams accompanying this part of the work are extremely interesting, especially those covering the region of Yorktown and Fredericksburg."—N. Y. TIMES.

JOMINI'S
ART OF WAR.

THE ART OF WAR. By Baron D. Jomini, General and Aid-de-Camp of the Emperor of Russia. A New Edition, with Appendices and Maps. Translated from the French by Capt. G. H. Mendell, U.S.A., Corps of Topographical Engineers, and Lieut. W. P. Craighill, U.S.A., Corps of Engineers.

One vol. demi 8vo. $1.50.

SUMMARY OF CONTENTS.

Chap. I.—Policy of War. II. Military Policy or the Philosophy of War. III. Strategy. IV. Grand Tactics and Battles. V. Of Different mixed Operations which participate at the same time of Strategy and Tactics. VI. Logistics, or the Practical art of moving Armies. VII. The Formation and Employment of Troops for Combat. Conclusion. SUPPLEMENT. APPENDICES.

MARMONT'S
MILITARY INSTITUTIONS.

THE SPIRIT OF MILITARY INSTITUTIONS, from the latest Paris edition. Translated, with Notes, by Henry Coppee, Professor in the University of Pennsylvania, and late a Captain in the Army of the United States. 1 vol. 12mo. $1.00.

This book contains, in a small compass, the principles of the art of war, as learned and practiced by this great marshal during the Napoleonic wars. It treats of strategy, tactics, and grand tactics; of the organization and formation of armies; the principles of fortification; of military justice; wars offensive and defensive; marches and encampments, reconnoissances, battles; and various important topics, including the tactics of the three arms, as applied in actual movements before the enemy,—with the peculiar characteristics and duties of general officers.

INSTRUCTION IN FIELD ARTILLERY.

Prepared by a Board of Artillery Officers.

ONE VOL. 8vo. $2.50.

BALTIMORE, MD., Jan. 15, 1859.

Col. S. COOPER, Ad't.-Gen. U.S.A.

Sir:—The Light Artillery Board assembled by Special Orders No. 134, of 1856, and Special Orders No. 116, of 1858, has the honor to submit a revised system of Light Artillery Tactics and Regulations recommended for that arm.

WM. H. FRENCH, *Bt. Major, Capt. First Artillery.*
WILLIAM F. BARRY, *Capt. Second Artillery.*
HENRY J. HUNT, *Bt. Major, Capt. Second Artillery.*

CAVALRY TACTICS.

PUBLISHED BY ORDER OF THE WAR DEPARTMENT.

First Part:

School of the Trooper; of the Platoon and of the Squadron Dismounted.

Second Part:

Of the Platoon and of the Squadron mounted.

Third Part:

Evolutions of a Regiment.

Three Vols. 18mo. $3.50.

WAR DEPARTMENT, *Washington*, Feb. 10, 1841.

The system of Cavalry Tactics adapted to the organization of Dragoon regiments, having been approved by the President of the United States, is now published for the government of the said service.

Accordingly, instruction in the same will be given after the method pointed out therein; and all additions to or departures from the exercises and manœuvres laid down in this system are positively forbidden.

J. R. POINSETT, *Secretary of War.*

100

UNITED STATES

INFANTRY TACTICS:

FOR THE INSTRUCTION, EXERCISE, AND MAN-
ŒUVRES OF THE U. S. INFANTRY, including Infantry of the Line, Light Infantry, and Riflemen. Prepared under the direction of the War Dapartment, and
authorized and adopted by SIMON CAMERON, Secretary of
War. Containing The School of the Soldier; The School
of the Company; Instruction for Skirmishers; The General Calls; The Calls for Skirmishers, and the School of
the Battalion; including a Dictionary of Military Terms.
One volume, complete illustrated with numerous Engravings. $1.25.

WAR DEPARTMENT, *Washington*, May 1, 1861.
This System of United States Infantry Tactics for Light Infantry
and Riflemen, prepared under the direction of the War Department,
having been approved by the President, is adopted for the instruction
of the troops when acting as Light Infantry or Riflemen, and, under
the act of May 12, 1820, for the observance of the militia when so employed.   SIMON CAMERON, *Secretary of War.*

INSTRUCTIONS FOR

OUTPOST AND PATROL DUTY.

Instructions for Officers and Non-commissioned Officers or
Outpost and Patrol Duty, with

THE SKIRMISH DRILL

for Mounted Troops. Authorized and adopted by the
Secretary of War, Sept. 2d, 1861. Price 25 cents.

* * * * All Colonels, and others in authority, will see
it that their commands are instructed in these duties. * * * *
SIMON CAMERON, *Secretary of War.*

POWER'S
ANATOMY OF THE ARTERIES.

ANATOMY OF THE ARTERIES OF THE HUMAN
Body, Descriptive and Surgical, with the Descriptive
Anatomy of the Heart. By JOHN HATCH POWER,
M.D., Fellow of the Royal College of Surgeons, Sur-
geon to the City of Dublin Hospital, etc. etc. 12mo,
amply illustrated. $2.00.

TREATISE ON MILITARY HYGIENE.

A TREATISE ON HYGIENE, WITH SPECIAL REF-
erence to the Military Service. By WILLIAM A.
HAMMOND, M. D., Surgeon-General U. S. Army.
[In Press.]

HOSPITAL STEWARD'S MANUAL.

THE HOSPITAL STEWARD'S MANUAL: A Book
of Instruction for Hospital Stewards, Ward Masters,
and Attendants in their several duties. Prepared in
strict accordance with existing regulations and the
customs of service in the armies of the United States
of America. By JOSEPH JANVIER WOODWARD, M.D.,
Assistant Surgeon U.S.A. 12mo. $1.25.

GUTHRIE'S

SURGERY OF WAR.

——— ❖ ———

COMMENTARIES ON THE SURGERY OF THE WAR

IN PORTUGAL, SPAIN, FRANCE, AND THE NETHERLANDS,

From the battle of Rolica, in 1808, to that of Waterloo, in
1815, with additions relating to those in the CRIMEA,
in 1854–55; showing the improvements made during and
since that period in the great art and science of Surgery
on all the subjects to which they relate.

BY G. J. GUTHRIE, F.R.S.

One vol. 12mo.   Price $2.25.

[FROM THE PREFACE TO THE SIXTH LONDON EDITION.]

"The rapid sale of the fifth, and the demand for a sixth edition of
this work, enable me to say that the precepts inculcated in it have
been fully borne out and confirmed by the practice of the Surgeons
of the Army in the Crimea in almost every particular.   *   *   *
They have performed operations of the greatest importance, at my
suggestion, that had not been done before, with a judgment and ability beyond all praise; and they have modified others, to the great
advantage of those who may hereafter suffer from similar injuries.

❊   ❊   ❊   ❊   ❊   ❊   ❊   ❊

"The precepts laid down are the result of the experience acquired
in the war in the Peninsula, from the first battle of Roliça, in 1808, to
the last in Belgium, of Waterloo, in 1815, which altered, nay, over-
turned, nearly all those which existed previously to that period, on
all the points to which they relate,—points as essential in the surgery of domestic as in military life.   They have been the means of
saving the lives, and of relieving, if not even of preventing, the miseries of thousands of our fellow-creatures throughout the civilized
world."

MACLEOD'S
SURGERY OF THE CRIMEAN WAR.

NOTES ON THE SURGERY OF THE WAR IN THE CRIMEA, with Remarks on the Treatment of Gunshot Wounds. By GEORGE H. B. MACLEOD, M.D., F.R.C.S., Surgeon to the General Hospital in Camp before Sebastopol, Lecturer on Military Surgery in Anderson's University, Glasgow, etc. etc.

One vol. 12mo. $1.50.

SUMMARY OF CONTENTS.